THE CULL OF
PERSONALITY

THE CULL OF PERSONALITY

Ayahuasca, Colonialism, and the Death of a Healer

Kevin Tucker

© Kevin Tucker, 2019.

ISBN: 978-0-9972017-7-2

Black and Green Press
PO Box 402
Salem, MO 65560

kevintucker.org
blackandgreenpress.org

Layout and design by Black and Green Press.

Printed in Canda on recycled paper.

The tragedy of Indian cultures is not their vanishing, it is the misery of the societies they enter, a tragedy in which we are also trapped.
-Janet Siskind, *To Hunt in the Morning*[1]

Dedicated to Olivia Arévalo and
to all who have and will continue to fight.

For Yank, Mica and Dyani.

CONTENTS

A Shallow Grave   1

The Death of a Healer   6

People of the Ucayali   20

Recurring Nightmares   42

Visions of Silent Despair   75

What Becomes of the Broken   120

Acknowledgements   167

Endnotes   169

Bibliography   186

The Shallow Grave

As civilization spreads and deepens, it is ultimately man's self, his species being, which is imperialized.
-Stanley Diamond, *In Search of the Primitive*[2]

A shocking amount of history can fit into a shallow grave.

The wake of civilization is a trail of bodies rotting over decimated landscapes. Reduced from the cycles of life, infinite needs clash violently with a finite world. A trembling craving becomes the colonizer's justification before the anchors lift and the swords are even brandished. Scorched earth. Manifest destiny. Development, by any other name, all comes down to ceaseless extraction.

For Peru, that trail had a strong precedent.

In fourteen hundred ninety two, Columbus sailed the ocean blue. The wayward explorer set off for the Indies, stubbornly believing for the entirety of his life that this is where he had gone. That didn't stop the Crowns of Castile-Aragón (later to become Spain) and Portugal

1

from signing the treaty at Tordesillas. In doing so, they divided and staked their claims to the territory before Columbus set sail again in 1494.[3]

Seeking a new, direct trade route to Asia, Columbus and the Crowns he represented were perfectly happy sticking to the plunder of gold instead. Of course he didn't stop there. He gloated on his first voyage how easily his men could conquer and enslave entire Indigenous populations.

On his second trip, he successfully tested that theory by enslaving 1,500 of the Taino people. Most of them were sent to La Isabel in the Dominican Republic, Europe's first city of the New World. Of those, 550 were sent all the way back to Seville to the Castile-Aragón Kingdom.[4]

The arteries of the New World were now, quite literally, open.

As Vasco Nuñez de Balboa forcibly crossed the Isthmus of Panama in 1513, Francisco Pizarro was in his ranks. Meanwhile, Hernán Cortés began tearing through Mexico in 1519. Two years later, he destroyed the Aztec capital of Tenochtitlan.

1530, Pizarro leads his own expedition out to take Peru. Three years later, the Inca capital of Cuzco is under his command.[5]

The bravado of the conqueror would have let their egos take total credit for the utter and absolute desolation that comes along with this very brief timeline. However, there was an unintended assist: disease. Smallpox makes its first appearance alongside Cortés' horde in 1518. By 1525, it had already spread to and wrought havoc among the Incas. A catastrophic blow to the native Peruvians, this is the wave that Pizarro rode in on.

Smallpox was hardly alone. Over the next half of the century, measles, typhus, and influenza are added to the mix. While the death toll of these diseases alone is nearly impossible to isolate, the best estimates, in the valley of Mexico alone, are that the population went from twenty-five million, prior to contact, down to one million by 1600.[6]

Had disease not cleared the way, Pizarro—armed only with 167 men—likely would have never taken Cuzco and claimed Peru.[7] Not for lack of trying, at least. Bartolomé de Las Casas spoke of Pizarro and his men like all of the other colonizers of the time: perverse butchers. They used dogs to rip people apart as they burned down houses and settlements. They tore babies from their mother's breasts to see how far they could throw them.[8]

Las Casas, however, was more concerned with what he seemed to believe was a more demented tactic of Pizarro. After having extracted all of the gold and silver, after having enslaved and forced the servitude of the Peruvians, when he felt that they had nothing left to give him, he would hold a small ritual and proclaim the enslaved as subjects of the Crown and that they were now under its protection. With this proclamation, he could act as though all of the domination, torture, enslavement, and decimation had occurred outside the realm of the Spanish Crown.

In this act, he was able to completely wash his hands of it all.[9]

We become numb to all of this. Even in Las Casas' accounts, there's almost a Biblical sense of lethargic passivity: massive and grotesque displays of inhumane cruelty almost feel normal. Just like an act of a jealous and vengeful God. The very same God that both Las Casas and Pizarro felt they were acting on behalf of.

Hundreds of years later, it becomes almost passé to speak of the colonization of the Americas. We're even less likely to look to the entirety of the Southern hemisphere as it was taken by a collection of desperate and hungry European empires, beginning around 1400. It becomes even more cumbersome to point towards the militant expansion of farmers and herders for thousands of years prior out of the Middle East and parts of Asia.

There's enough implicit Western chauvinism to cover for the expanding mound building nation-states of Uto-Aztecans and their progeny occurring in the Americas at that same time. The conquered Maya and Inca were well versed enough in conquest that if disease were removed from the equation, it's doubtful that European invaders would have had the numbers or technology to claim the New World as their own.

We remove ourselves from all of this because we consider it history. We speak of colonization in the past tense. In hindsight, it all becomes an event. We get a start date and an end point. We mark it with landmarks and fill museums. Statues posthumously give murderers another pedestal to stand upon.

A butcher like Pizarro becomes the iconic colonizer. Loved or hated, he becomes a period piece of sorts, a symbol.

In this, history grants us the permission to reenact the one thing that seemed to truly catch Las Casas off guard: the ability of Pizarro to wash his hands of his own actions. Because the reality of our world is that colonization is the on-going side effect of unchecked and potentially unstoppable growth.

From the dawn of civilization, this is the world that domestication has demanded. That is, a world where entitlement is the unquestioned virtue of might. In isolating ourselves in a present separated from our own past, we no longer have to answer for the trajectories that led our reality to collide with the ancient world we all exist within. All of its relationships and feedback loops become the uncredited, off-screen deaths of a play we already considered over.

We are living civilization. That means our existence is inextricable from colonization.

It means that nothing is said and done yet. Nothing is over.

Pizarro, like the other infamous conquistadors, becomes emblematic. We know what they look like. We have our opinions about them, but those books are written. In their own way, that narrative closes us off from the legacy that Pizarro, Columbus, Cortés, and Balboa typified.

But that shallow grave? It's not for Pizarro. His remains sit in boxes enshrined in an altar. One that lays in a Catholic cathedral in Lima, Peru: a continual reminder of the right of conquest over the colonized.[10] The decimated. There it remains, the ghost of a manifested destiny in the heart of its spreading cancer.

The shallow grave I'm concerned with, this particular one, belonged to a Canadian man: 41-year-old Sebastian Woodroffe.

Separated by roughly 450 miles and 477 years, it is no less a reminder of the reality of colonization than the entombed and displayed remains of Pizarro.

The Death of a Healer

Every last passenger pigeon, of a population of
birds that once blackened the skies, was killed by a
people who do not find in themselves the necessity
to think about the relationship of pigeons to man,
the future, the land.
-John Mohawk, 'In Search of Noble Ancestors'[11]

Sebastian Woodroffe, we are meant to believe, had good intentions. Honorable even.

At the very least, he is largely given the benefit of the doubt. That is, to the world outside of the village where he died: Victoria Garcia, Peru. There, his remains are much less significant than those of Maestra Olivia Arévalo.

And rightfully so.

At 81, Arévalo's reputation as a healer had outgrown the village where Woodroffe found her. If *The Guardian* is to be believed, she has been hailed as a "spiritual mother of the Shipibo-Konibo."[12] Her role as a respected *Onanya*, a plant medicine healer, was well known.

The Shipibo-Conibo are a complicated culture. Despite being the second largest tribe in the Peruvian Amazon, information is surprisingly hard to come by. But to understand why that is, it's important to know the primary reason they erupted into the larger consciousness of a technologically infused and hyper-modernized world, then subsequently onto Woodroffe's radar: *ayahuasca.*

Ayahuasca refers to a number of hallucinogenic brews made involving *Banisteriopsis caapi*, a native plant in the Amazon. The name is a Quechua word, meaning "the vine of souls."[13] There are a number of combinations made in making ayahuasca, but a common one uses the leaves of plants in the *Psychotria* genus. The brew contains the hallucinogenic compound dimethyltryptamine, DMT, released from the *Psychotria*, potentiated by *Banisteriopsis.*[14] In the United States, DMT is a Schedule 1 narcotic. In Peru, it is legal.

It has also come to play an important part in the spiritual world of many Amazonian tribes.

Throughout the Amazonian region, a number of cultures treat it differently. Mixed with other plants, some use the bark in a cold-water infusion, some boil the bark and stems, in some places the fresh bark is chewed, and in others, a snuff is made. Some have no interest in it at all.

Not all methods are equally powerful, but ayahuasca is exceptionally potent. In all variations, "partakers often 'experience' death and the separation of body and soul."[15] Boiling seems to produce the strongest results. But all forms are prone to violent and unpleasant aftereffects. Its consumption is followed by nausea and vomiting. Painful and discomforting, there's little about experiencing death that should give any indication of being enjoyable.

The sickness, if doses are correct, should be followed by a pleasant euphoria paired with visual hallucinations. Taken in excess, the user is subjected to "frighteningly nightmarish visions" and "a feeling of extremely reckless abandon." However, losing consciousness is rare and nothing inhibits movement.[16]

So if you're following along, then you may recognize that this can be a particularly dangerous combination. Nightmarish visions while the user is fully conscious and capable of movement.

It becomes immediately obvious why someone like Arévalo becomes so highly regarded. Ayahuasca, culturally speaking, is not a recreational thing. Its power is well known and respected, which is why its use can be so heavily shrouded in ritual. It's also why having a time-tested healer like Arévalo is so important.

Ayahuasca, it should go without saying, is a part of a larger cultural context.

Unfortunately so is Peru.

In Victoria Garcia on April 19, 2018, that larger global context looked like Woodroffe. He drove his motorcycle to Arévalo's home, carrying the .380 semi-automatic pistol that he bought off a police officer just over two weeks prior.

There, in the middle of the day, he shot Arévalo twice.

She died in the arms of her daughter.[17]

Woodroffe, as he saw it, was in Peru to save lives.

His trips were covered in part by a Kickstarter campaign, parts of which now feel particularly ironic:

> *As old ideas meet the new, it is natural that they run into each other a little bit before melding and helping each other get stronger. I wish to be a part of this process, to make it happen.*[18]

They definitely ran into each other and he was unquestionably a part of that process. But the entirety of it is massive. That process is far larger and deeper than Woodroffe was likely ever to see, particularly while on ayahuasca.

Arévalo, however, had to have been far less shocked.

Woodroffe might have been her last encounter with soul-searching Westerners on the front-line of colonization, but he was definitely not her first.

Ayahuasca, as Woodroffe and others like him see it, is healing. Period.

Particularly, he believed, it could be extremely useful in overcoming addiction and post-traumatic stress disorder (PTSD). He wasn't alone in this. Arévalo's name likely crossed his path because she was briefly employed by Temple of the Way of Light: a place that sounds like it was named by an online random cult name generator.

The Temple, located near Iquitos, Peru, specializes in Ayahuasca-based healing retreats. There, the much-vaunted healing powers of the vine are given the resort-casual variation. "Shamans" of the Shipibo are employed as guides. You can read about it in their promotional materials.

From 2009 to 2011, that included Arévalo.[19]

According to their website, "healing retreats are

intense, typically with deep insights and profound restoration taking place in a short amount of time." Very efficient: very convenient. The Temple sits on 175 hectares of rain forest, features a permaculture center, a kitchen run on solar energy, and spring-fed drinking water. Lest the Western visitors be concerned, there is running water for showers, electricity, and 24-hour access to nearby medical facilities.

If you need further assurance, the Temple also won Retreat.guru's "Safe Ayahuasca Retreat" Award in 2015, 2016, and 2017. I'm not sure what any of that is or even could be worth, but I would be remiss if I didn't follow that up with a reminder that this is a real website and business. There are also apparently enough ayahuasca retreats to merit awards.

At the Temple, programs range from $2,100 to $2,950, from a 9-day stay up to an extensive 23-day retreat. The 23-day retreat is more drawn out, focused on a New Age grab bag of appropriated and mimicked practices, doused in a faux-spiritualism, featuring yoga, meditation, and art therapy. The 14-day program shifts a bit more into a different realm of the self-help world, adding "self-inquiry" to the ayahuasca, yoga, and meditation. This includes, in their words, "a comprehensive program of progressive therapeutic and Eastern psycho-spiritual practices." The 11-day Alignment Intensive program mixes ayahuasca "with ontological inquiry."[20] Again, these are their words.

It would be reassuring to say that the Temple is a one of a kind huckster scheme. It is far from it. I have no reason to believe that Woodroffe even knew of the Temple at all, or this Temple anyway. Ayahuasca retreats are far from a cottage industry in Peru, they're a full-blown tourist destination. Thousands of Westerners go there annually to dip their psyche in the psycho-spiritual waters of "authentic" healing.

According to Retreat.guru, there are 241 retreat centers in Peru. Of those, it would appear that most of them specialize in ayahuasca. Each center tries to appear more appealing and some even more authentic than the others. If you're looking for a shamanic apprentice program, but want to have your own catered room and be served vegan food, there's an option for that. If you want to take part in a permaculture program and detox from your technology, there's an option for that as well.

Which program Woodroffe took part in during his five years of traveling on and off in Peru really doesn't matter. In the scheme of things, Woodroffe is hardly unique. In fact, it is in the lackluster aspects of Woodroffe's trip that we see just how widespread and insidious the entirety of the ayahuasca-tourism industry really is.

He's not even the only Westerner to die.

Over the last decade, eleven Westerners died in ayahuasca-related events in South America. You have some who died of complications in taking the drug itself—it is not uncommon for it to be mixed with other drugs—but you have murder as well. In 2015, a former Goldman Sachs analyst grabbed a knife during an ayahuasca ceremony and attacked a Canadian man. The Canadian acted in self-defense and the analyst died in the struggle. There's that mix of nightmarish visions and uninhibited movement for you.

Despite all of this, the tourism industry keeps on growing.

Once the fascination of fringe-adventure journalists like those at Vice, celebrities of all stripes are singing praises of the healing powers of their ayahuasca retreats. Peru is becoming the destination of choice for high profile corporate pawns, much like that former Goldman Sachs analyst.[21]

Woodroffe echoed all of that.

The problem is that it sounds, on the whole, pretty good. After having a run-in with addiction in his own family, Woodroffe was appalled by the dismal state of existing addiction recovery programs. And rightfully so: just not for reasons that Woodroffe was likely to ever understand.

Addiction and civilization go hand in hand.[22]

The domestication process that is the core of a civilized existence is about disrupting our needs as social animals and channeling them back through a culture so bereft of meaning that we are willing to bite onto any meager alternative that we are sold. And there are many, including sipping on a vomit-inducing vine-based hallucinatory brew.

It is the consumptive nature of this late era of capitalism that convinces us that the piece of ourselves that we are missing, the one that keeps us constantly chasing after something, anything, is for sale. Most of us, we believe, just haven't found it. Or we just can't afford it. Yet.

The reality is that we are living in the hyper-technological, electronically emerged world of Progress that our parents and their parents dreamed of. That is a dream that they were sold. A dream they bought and worked for.

And it is a dream that offers no fulfillment.

We have everything at our disposal. That is, those of us with First World privileges. Yet depression continues to skyrocket. The opioid epidemic grows with no sign of slowing. The world feels like it's burning and in our personalized technological feedback loops, we just keep feeding the fire.

What do you do? Medications are the short sell. People grind themselves down to pay for health insurance to cover the expenses related to the stress of not being able to afford it and physical decline comes along for the ride. We aren't force fed garbage, but we overindulge in it as if we were. We live sedentary, isolated lives in a sea of untold radiation and toxins.

Perhaps it is most telling that every year since 2014 has seen a reduction of the average life expectancy among Americans. The fastest growing causes of death? Suicide, overdose, and accident. Increasingly, the Center for Disease Control is considering all three to be one category, and rightfully so. All three are linked in an overall and growing sense of disinterest in life that embraces the possibility of doing dangerous and potentially fatal things, often riding the line between passive and active suicide.[23]

There's an unending list, but there's no point in reciting it all here. Woodroffe, and many others like him, didn't and don't need to ask questions about whether or not depression and addiction were issues. Neither do I. Clearly they are. Clearly currently available solutions haven't seemed to cure anyone or anything.

12-step programs, scale-down narcotics, recovery centers: Woodroffe knew these weren't the solution. But in his mind, and apparently many others, the answer wasn't in looking at the cause of the problems: it was in the programs.

The logic is simple. And simplistic.

It goes like this: there is a depth of knowledge, another plane of consciousness, which holds universal truths. Ayahuasca, as well as other hallucinogenic plants like it, grant us quicker access to that truth. They offer a magical mirror in which we can see both our problems and ourselves more clearly. We need to heal and this is a sacred path that we need to be taking.

For Woodroffe and his spiritual mentors, it's not our circumstances, it's our attitude: our approach.

We just need to see the bigger picture.

In the words of another one of ayahuasca's promoters and a preacher of some kind of shamanic truth: "there are other ways, other practices that can be used to gain access to the knowledge and wisdom one gains from Ayahuasca but with the plants, it's an accelerated curriculum, an accelerated course."[24] Enlightenment fast tracked.

There's a history to this thinking.

A romanticism that lives in *The Yage Letters*, a 1963 book collecting letters and writings exchanged between Allen Ginsberg and William S Burroughs. Yagé, another name given to ayahuasca, is the subject of travels and experimentation by the two notorious writers. They then upheld it for its world bending hallucinations.

That carries on into Carlos Castaneda's Don Juan books, published not long after. Seeking out the wholeness of a mythic Yaqui shaman and the spiritual oneness he holds. Oneness attained through the powers of peyote. Following soon after is Terrence McKenna and his reimagining of the world through the eyes of the hallucinogenic psilocybin mushroom.

To call this romanticism is to miss the point entirely.

It's not just romantic: it's reductionist.

This is the basis of an exploitive relationship. The cultural contexts all pushed aside, what that culture has are resources: an access point for mental liberation. A cure-all for depression, trauma, and addiction: one that doesn't require any kind of validation other than a whimsical nostalgia for what Castaneda thought Don Juan would be thinking.

Literally fiction.

Beneath all of this is a faux-back-to-the-land mysticism. A product of a generation that was willing to do anything to shake the moral and political rigidity that lay before them. Typified by one of the loudest proponents of psychedelics, Timothy Leary, the praxis was to "turn on, tune in, drop out."

There was a boiling cauldron of unhinged "Native American" spirituality that was cartoonish at best, but racist in hindsight. They might have meant well, but the reactionary, liberated imaginations needed no grounding other than whatever its advocates believed they found on some other plane of consciousness.

Some got it, most didn't.

Thomas King sums it up: Self-proclaimed hippies, flower children, and bums "made their way to reserves and reservations throughout North America, sure that Native peoples possessed the secret to life." They sought out something they didn't have.

What they found was poverty: "Or at least poverty was what they saw."[25]

Dismayed with native realities, they left. The mythical idealized "Indian" lived another day.

Still indulging the fantasy, whimsical Oneness—that other plane of consciousness—was still out there. They could get there with or without a cardboard variant of "shamanism," but they often relied on it anyway. This despite the fact that, at that very same time, just as now, there was a well-rooted and necessary attempt by native groups to actively resist genocidal policies and practices. These are governmental, corporate, religious, and social attempts to root out the natives and their traditions. No amount of headdresses, dream catchers, and grotesque efforts to "play Indian" were going to save that generation or confront that reality. If anything, they fed into it.

For whatever reason, the sentiment didn't die there. It just evolved.

But what enrages me most about that situation is that the sheer entitlement so often gets overlooked. Perhaps it's just the pervasiveness of overt racism against natives, from their derogatory use as sports mascots to the constant desecration of sacred places for mining or luxury resorts, or the fact that governments and frontier industries still publicly call for the extermination of the peoples themselves, but the reality of colonialism is still fully alive.

And it has many faces.

In 1895, Captain Richard Henry Pratt, the man who became superintendent of the Indian Industrial School in Carlisle, Pennsylvania, declared that it was the goal of the forced residential school program: to "kill the Indian, save the man."[26] In their charismatic upholding of a fantastical stereotype of native societies in the face of policies of extermination, the default of the hippies and psychedelic dreamers became "let the people die, but save the Indian."

That might seem like an exaggeration, which underlines the point: *but they meant well.*

So what has that done? What has tourism done for any native society? Brought roads and all that they entail? What has a cartoonish version of their culture, reduced to their dress and ritual, done for any of them?

We arrive at this point in this story because there is maliciousness, an almost blatant insidiousness, in the will that has been granted to Woodroffe and people like him.

Again, in his own words:

I cannot stress how important it can be to retain old knowledge such as the knowledge these people have harboured in there [sic] *cultural memory. It is a far more valuable resource than all the trees, minerals, and oil in the whole Amazon.*[27]

These people have harbored.

Like a fugitive, there is a universal truth that *they* have access to. One that, ostensibly, *we* deserve. Their cultural memory is ours to mine, drill, and take away.

Had Woodroffe one ounce of decency or genuine care for the Shipibo, as a people, he would have done a little bit of homework before declaring their cultural memory a resource. If he had, he would see that they, like all Indigenous people, have always been seen as a resource. Their lives measured in value against all the trees, minerals, and oils in the Amazon and everywhere else throughout the entire world.

His statement, like the realities he thought ayahuasca would open up, was never based on an objective truth, but a self-centered urge. He wanted to heal. He wanted to be a healer. He was in Peru to save a cultural memory of a plant—one that grew thousands of miles away—from the people who still lived alongside it.

It's hard to contain my anger, but hindsight only makes his words sting worse. "Cultural knowledge," he states plainly, "cannot be restored once it is wiped out. It is something that takes tens of thousands of years to nurture."

These are the words of a man who killed an *onanya*, a woman who wasn't just among the most notorious healers, but also a staunch advocate for Shipibo-Konibo rights. He came to her because she had songs that she sang during the healing rituals. Sacred songs. *Her songs*.

And he demanded them.

She said no.

He had purchased a gun. He brought it with him. There are many sketchy details here. Many that weren't clear. But there were witnesses. And because they too are natives, those accounts don't seem to matter much to the colonizer's narrative.

"I feel responsible trying to support this culture," says Woodroffe, again speaking without any self awareness, "and retain some of their treasure in me and my family, and share it with those that wish to learn."[28]

Me and my family.

He pulls the trigger. Point blank.

Twice.

Woodroffe's friends would later say that he was the wrong man. He would never do this. This isn't who he is. This isn't what he is capable of. Never mind that the trips and ayahuasca seemed to make him more distant and to act a bit off. He was a father. He wanted to heal.

He could not be a murderer.

In their eyes, all the witnesses were too native to know the difference between Woodroffe and any other white guy. Never mind that his clothes had residue from the gun he shot point blank, the gun he purchased and brought with him.

He meant well.

There is no version of this story where Arévalo lives. None where Woodroffe comes to his senses and realizes the pit of history, the colonial frontier, that he is standing in as he holds a gun to an 81 year old healer. A healer that *he* sought out and is making demands of.

Every telling, every variant, and every fantasy of his supposed innocence: she is still dead.

After Pizarro bled the Incans dry, after exploiting them to bring him all of their precious metals, after having turned over other natives for slaves, after having cleared the land and burned their villages, he washed his hands of it all.

In his telling of the story, by the end, he was there to protect the people.

Civilization demands a specific pathology, rooted in the stunted development that domestication requires. In it, the cognitive dissonance between action and responsibility can be worlds apart. *It had to be done.* It might be ugly, but colonization is the reality of a civilized existence.

That is what we tell ourselves.

That is how Woodroffe, in the minds of many, gets to be the victim, if not the hero.

And Arévalo dies every time.

The People of the Ucayali

*The arrival of the Leviathan set off crashing waves
of violence all around.*
- R Brian Ferguson, 'The Blood of Leviathan'[29]

It is impossible to understand the enormity of Arévalo's
murder without the larger context.

"The Amazon has long had a frontier economy,
based on the exploitation of its natural resources," this
is coming from Ana Echazu-Boschemeier, an anthropologist in Brazil. She continues: "shamanic tourism
is replicating this savage logic of extractive industries
where people and nature have little protection."[30]

In word and in action, it's hard not to see Woodroffe's firm place in that lineage.

Though Arévalo might have been killed over ayahuasca, it takes some work and digging to really understand how the vine even grew into the picture. Here,
history runs deep. Within it, the Shipibo are almost like
a phantom skirting the edges. We get mere glimpses of
them more than anything.

The archaeological record indicates that human occupation along the Ucayali River and its tributaries goes back at least 4000 years. That's an estimate likely to be far too modest. The region is cut by the Andes Mountains, potentially one reason why the Shipibo weren't speaking Quechua, like the Inca.

The Shipibo are Pano speakers. While ethnographic and explorer accounts tend to collide over who was where and when, the names that circulate within this particular region are largely the Shipibo, Conibo, Campa (who speak Arawak), and Cocoma. Along the Ucayali, distinct Panoan ceramics start to appear around 300 AD.[31]

It had been presumed that the shared language and, quite often, cultural similarities tied the Panoan speakers into one larger cultural complex, but it is increasingly obvious that this is not the case.[32] History brought a great number of changes and shifts for the Panoans, but there is enough hostility between them—likely dating back prior to European conquest—not to insult them by lumping them all together.

Despite sometimes having areas of overlap, the groups kept a good bit of distance between each other. The Ucayali River's occupants kept buffer zones between each other. In less violent times, this should have helped keep tensions down, but it also happens to create an ecological reservoir of sorts. An unclaimed region between territories.[33]

Regardless, the groups all bump into the historical record definitively in the seventeenth century. Even from there, it is often spotty, at best. Where there is a collision though is extremely vital. To understand that, it's important to dig more into Peru and the Amazon after European contact.

The Inca Empire has its origins in the mid-1400s. Not long before Europeans drove their swords into the Americas, not long after the Mayan civilization to the north had collapsed.

For Pizarro, after seeing the glory that Cortés got from decimating the remaining Maya, the Inca were the next big target.

At that time, the Spanish Empire had fostered the colonizers decimating the continent, but the Empire itself was less concerned with micromanaging the conquest. Cortés, for example, invaded and conquered Mexico without authorization from the Spanish throne. The king and queen wondered aloud about what to do with their newly inherited 'subjects.' Not that there was an ounce more compassion coming from the royalty; the options they proposed were whether the Indigenous societies should be kept as slaves or subjected to conversion to Christianity and made citizens.[34]

While the Crown was making its decisions, slavery remained the default. Colonialism was left largely to the colonizers themselves. Or groups like the Jesuits, for whom the Society of Jesus was a significant landowner itself. The Jesuit missionaries graciously claimed the land surrounding any missions that they had built.

Throughout the 1500s, Spanish America "was a territorial empire controlled by a tiny European minority."[35] Until his death, that included Pizarro.

As we've seen, the legacy of enslaving natives goes back to Columbus' second journey. That would set a major theme for the rest of history in the Americas. But disease wiping out so much of the native population didn't sway the colonizers from their slave-fueled plans. Pizarro and his family received over 250 licenses to import slaves in the first years of conquest alone.[36]

Slaves became immediately crucial to Peru's standing in the global economy. Lima became one of the largest slave ports in the world.[37] When Spain passed the New Laws of 1542—laws meant to end the enslavement of Native Americans—the Peruvian colonizers were so enraged that they decapitated the official the Crown had sent to enforce them.[38]

The New Laws meant little to nothing.

Not in the frontier. Not when so much power and control had already been established in the world of the conquerors themselves. They simply changed the way things were worded, establishing an *encomienda* system, where colonists were granted land and the right to the Indigenous peoples on it. It's a system that spreads way too far into the present.

Within years, Peru was importing massive numbers of slaves and exporting textiles, minerals, metals, and sugar back to Europe. In that regard, things haven't changed much. Contemporary Peru is the fifth largest exporter of gold (first in Latin America), second in copper, and in the top five on lead and zinc. Iron ore, coal, phosphate, potash and natural gas are high on the list.

And, of course, there's timber.

The slopes of the Andes are particularly steep. This had kept some degree of logging at bay in the region, but not by much. Every year, more of the Amazon is cut at a grotesque rate. The ports of Lima and their ships demanded a lot of wood, so it was cut. Considering that upwards of 40% of the Mayan lowlands were secondary growth, it is obvious that native civilizations were no less resource hungry.[39] There is no reason to believe the

Inca were less inclined to consume the forests either.

This is the stage the Shipibo would unwittingly enter onto: a world ruled by conquerors.

This is a world that ran on slavery.

Here things start to get a bit more complicated.

Warfare, raiding, and slavery were far from a European import, even though slavery became a lucrative European export. While the Panoan speakers and their neighbors might have had a number of significant cultural differences, a major similarity was their subsistence. They were all slash and burn horticulturalists: gardeners who hunt and gather.

Prior to contact, the Shipibo were planting cassava and plantains. They hunted manatees and caiman with spears. They hunted with blow darts, but it's hard to say how long this went on or if it had changed. The blowguns, darts, and poison were all bought or traded from the neighboring Yagua. Bows and arrows came after contact as well.[40]

Like other horticulturalists, they also had warfare.[41]

This led to patterns of war, raiding, and enslavement that caused a massive amount of flux as to which society was where and when.[42] There are a number of reasons for that, but it's important to note that the notion of "tribes" here is largely a colonial and historical creation. Speaking of a relative neighbor, "there is no evidence to suggest that Asháninka [Campa] constituted a 'tribe'—that is, a circumscribed, corporate, ethnolinguistic group—in any meaningful sense prior to European contact."[43]

How much these patterns were created, shifted, or amplified by past relationships with the Inca is hard to say definitively. But it isn't hard to presume that there was considerable impact, just as we see massive and endemic change flooding in with European contact.

Further down the Ucayali River, we know that the Machiguenga (Campa) and Piro were involved with both raiding and trade with the Inca. It's worth noting that the two weren't necessarily exclusionary. Though the Inca never established an Andean state in the tropical forest region, there is no reason to believe that the Asháninka and their Panoan speaking neighbors wouldn't have maintained similar ties.[44]

If the Aztecs are any indication of how the Inca related to surrounding societies, then expansion and theft of people didn't demand a long-term territorial presence in order to pillage and plunder.[45]

Pillage and plunder, however, became seemingly constant.

This, in part, helps to explain why the "recorded history of the Shipibo is largely a record of their relations with other tribes and of their contacts with white men who entered the area."[46] That means that we get snapshots of periods of transition. In the early 1600s, that looked like the Campa forcing the Cashibo to the upper Aguayita River (tributary of the Ucayali). This pushed the Shipibo further towards the mouth of the river, displacing the Conibo in the process.[47]

Raids beget more raids. Lines get blurred.

From the late seventeenth century on, the Conibo were "inveterate raiders."[48] Marauders even. The primary target was the capture of women and children: women to become wives, girls as future wives, and boys to become slaves or servants.

The timing of the raids was often non-coincidental:

the dry season and into the early rainy season. That is peak harvest season. Not content to just steal people, they stole their produce too, allowing them to live off of the harvest of pillaged gardens. They literally took the clothes from the backs of the pillaged: preferring theft to weaving themselves.[49]

Conibo men were polygynous patriarchs. More women were taken as wives, who in turn would handle both agricultural production and reproduction. Namely the growing of manioc and maize: primarily to be turned into alcohol. "And in an Amazonian context, beer indeed made the world go round."[50]

There's no way to make light of it: this was full-on enslavement. At puberty, girls were subjected to clitoridectomies. The idea is a familiar one: in the eyes of the Conibo, "the surgical removal of the clitoris converted potentially wild and sexually voracious girls into more manageable and civilized wives."[51]

No one was prepared to just take this abuse. Remo women systematically committed infanticide on their children when conceived through rape and would often commit suicide to avoid further subjugation.[52]

But in the words and deeds of the Conibo, they were out to save the neighboring savages. To redeem them: pull them from their supposed backwards ways and make them respectable.

If it sounds like Pizarro, it should.

This is where the waters are most muddy. There is no doubt that the patterns of raiding and warfare predate European contact. Some might have even existed prior to Incan contact.

What is definite is that none of the pre-contact patterns looked anything like they did in a world of guns, steel axes, and international geopolitics—not in scale, not in occurrence, and not in practice.

This became a world defined and decimated by colonizers and conquest.

Let me state this with absolute clarity: I don't say any of this because I believe war or slavery in any form is acceptable, but the degree to which everything above sounds no different than how the Europeans acted is because the Europeans created this situation.

They amplified it.

They paid for it.

They subsidized it.

Europeans were unequivocally "major players in this history."[53]

There is no place in this world where European technology and disease didn't cause nearly insurmountable rifts and tears in the fabric of the societies that lay ahead of their infectious, colonizing spread.

This is something we see throughout the world.

Warfare, amongst horticulturalists and settled hunter-collectors, can be a bloody affair. Nasty as it can be, it can also be an ecological reaction to a significant shift in how we, as humans, interact with the world.

The nomadic life of hunter-gatherer bands takes care of a lot of potential social and ecological tension. There's even less need for groups to be defined or definable. There's nothing to stake a definitive claim on land wise. There's no hierarchy to wield over other people. There's no surplus to hoard.

Movement keeps populations down; settlement gives room for them to pop up. Warfare, in raids, battles, and in a general culture upholding a warrior-ethos—including a preference for having boys, meaning higher rates of female infanticide—can check that, even without regular wars or raids. The problem is that it becomes a way of seeing the world, a way of explaining problems, which is easily preyed upon.

If people start dying without a clear cause, then witchcraft and sorcery are pretty solid cultural explanations. In simpler times, they work well enough.

The problem is that they don't scale. At all.

So in catastrophic situations, such as in 1644—seven years after the Jesuits contacted the Cocama and brought their diseases with them, resulting in the death of seventy percent of their population—things cascade quickly. During that period, the Cocama were regularly warring with the Shipibo, who contracted the diseases themselves. They then passed them on to other societies that had raided or were raided by them.[54]

"It was their germs," writes Alfred Crosby, "not these imperialists themselves, for all their brutality and callousness, that were chiefly responsible for sweeping aside the indigenes and opening the Neo-Europes to demographic takeover."[55]

It rolls downhill forever.

Each part of the colonial encounter just adds to this mix.

In the Pacific Northwest, warfare between the Tlingit, Haida, Tsimshian, Bella Coola, Nootka, Kwakiutl, and Coast Salish reached an unprecedented peak when trade with Europeans came into the fold. That expansion, including the consequential exile of Inuit cultures in the fallout, spread directly from access to the new resource of manufactured goods.[56]

On the east coast of North America, the introduction of the fur trade and fuel provided by the introduction of muskets, fed and empowered the Haudenosaunee as a political entity. This spurred the formalization of the Iroquois Confederacy, later to be declared an empire by the French. That process led to the extermination of both wildlife and other societies to corner the fur-to-trade-goods pipeline.[57]

In New Zealand, the introduction of the musket exploded another powder keg of previous tensions. As a result, between one quarter and one half of the entire Maori population was wiped out.[58]

Back in the Amazon, there was plenty of attention given to the case of Yanomami warfare. Used by the sociobiologist Napoleon Chagnon to showcase what he claimed was evidence of humanity's warring state of nature, the reality was a far grimmer exposé of colonization and the civilized view of the world.[59] The simultaneous introduction of disastrous disease and steel tools ignited a chain reaction of warfare.[60] Potentially older ideas, but now implemented with new and far more lethal weaponry. The relationship between warring and access to trade goods was direct.[61]

Heading back towards the Ucayali River, the introduction of steel tools among the Jivaro caused massive cultural shifts. Axes made clearing gardens and growing manioc easier, feeding a cycle of more manioc beer, more tools, and, therefore, more violence. Despite all the proselytizing and disgust of the Europeans, a particularly morbid fascination with a byproduct of Jivaro warfare–*tsantsas*, the shrunken-head war trophies[62]— became a highly valued trade good. This led to an unchecked increase in raiding, powered by new ammunition and reward.

At the peak of their value, one head was worth one gun.[63]

On the Ucayali, things were no different.

Colonization, with all of its demands and agents, came in waves and floods.

First there were the people: the slave traders and the missionaries, insofar as they can be distinguished. Then the land itself: mines and lumber. As the world of global farmers scaled up, the soil took the hit. In the mid-nineteenth century, fertilizing salvation came in the form of guano, bat feces. And with it, an influx of Chinese slaves to dredge the caves.[64] This was followed by one of the bloodiest eras of the region, the rubber boom.[65]

Throughout, missionaries come and missionaries go. The extractions continue unabated.

Beginning around the mid-1600s, we start to get a lot more fragments of these cultures. And it gets very violent. One thing becomes immediately clear: the earlier relationship that all the Panoan and neighboring groups had with the Inca and each other, one where raiding and trade were both in the realm of possibility, becomes a defining trait in how Europeans are seen.

Tolerance for Europeans seemingly came down to one thing: usefulness.

The loyalty demanded by both the Crown and the cross had absolutely no cultural basis here. In a mix of opportunism and defiance, the colonizers weren't an ideological issue, but either a pragmatic resource or an enemy. The failure of Europeans to understand that is the principle reason many of them died.

Or, in the case of the missionaries, this was the reason that they became martyred.

And missionaries almost always arrived and were executed first.

In the region, an early effort at sustained contact was among the Asháninka. Franciscan missionaries had founded a mission in a strategic position: in close proximity to Salt Mountain, a communal source of salt that was used by the Asháninka, Yanesha, Conibo, and Piro, as well as nearby Andean societies. The two priests to head the mission overstepped their place quickly in trying to introduce shame around polygamy.

For their efforts, they were killed when the mission was barely two years old.

Two years later, in 1640, a Dominican missionary tried to reestablish the mission. He eyed up Salt Mountain with hopes for potential gold. He also acted like many missionaries would at the time: no different than any of the colonizers. He stole cattle from nearby communities, killed a native headman, raped Asháninka women who had converted, and stole their children to be servants. So the Asháninka fled.[66]

Slavery had taken on a new meaning. Against the backdrop of genocidal loss in the face of disease, societies went into a free fall. Women became a resource to ensure that each group would reproduce. And those boys the Conibo had claimed through raiding as servants? They were sold to the Cocama for iron tools.[67]

Iron tools that came from Europeans, bought with slaves.

This is a constant theme, both surrounding the Ucayali River and throughout the rest of the world. Missionaries weren't just there alongside colonizers: they were active agents.

Those failed New Laws? In the late 1500s, just to the west along another tributary of the Ucayali, many of the natives that had survived the catastrophic spread of disease had been parceled out into the *encomienda* system which bypassed any of the "slave" terminology that was now legally forbidden. The reality was no different. In the *encomiendas*, the threats to stability were the loss of the native population to diseases, that the natives would quite often flee, and, a more common occurrence, take up armed revolt.

After a particularly harsh uprising in 1638, the Jesuits were called in to attempt to restore order.

The Jesuits, as they would say it, were there to save souls.

Some souls, it turns out, are just harder to save than others. Jesuit policy created *reducciones*, not too distant from or unrelated to the *encomiendas*: they were "mission communities in which fugitive and otherwise uncooperative Indian populations were resettled, counted and monitored, put to work, and inculcated into the mysteries of Catholicism."[68]

On the frontier, there was no room for the initial leniency that more contemporary missionaries offer. With the help of considerable outside and governmental aid, missionaries of the twentieth century and onward can bait the mission settlements with food rations, tools, clothes, sugar, and the like. The earlier frontier missions, largely in the form of *encomiendas* and *reducciones*, were working encampments. The missionaries weren't able or willing to support the population, encouraging them to act more like any other colonizer to keep the natives as a captive work force.

Or, as should be clear by now, as slaves.

The persistent threats of death, escape, and resistance, were all very real for the missionaries. Which is exactly how it should have been. At no point was anyone willingly subjecting themselves to the misery of salvation; particularly when it meant working the outposts of a land that the enslaved had memory of living in, and on their own terms. The whole system required a combination of decimation and force. To be effective, all alternatives had to be wiped out.

It is the nature of the frontier that most were wiped out. Decimation becomes the larger context.

The patterns of raiding and warfare amongst other natives worked out well for the missionaries. Overdrawn and overstretched, the missions and settlements rose and fell. Often even in fairly quick succession. This kept the missionaries short sighted. Head to the ground, they just needed to keep the numbers up at the current mission until it too fell. With so many natives dying or fleeing, that was a persistent issue.

The easiest solution was to also be opportunistic: to feed into that raiding culture and to use the trade relationships with neighboring societies to advance and amplify the cycles of war already underway.

To put that more bluntly, they flooded the region with disease and in that wake they added in two crucial new instruments—steel tools and guns—then they reaped the rewards of the chaos that unfolded.

The missionaries had other natives do their dirty work for them.

It is the tragic nature of geography that the natives enslaved in Jesuit *reducciones* along the Marañón River were so distant from the Conibo. By the 1680s, the Conibo had built armadas, traveling annually to the

Jesuits to trade slaves—often, in their case, Remo and Amahuaca—for tools, axes, and salt. The Jesuits put the captives into the *reducciones*, considering them *cimarrones*, "the escaped."[69]

They weren't. They couldn't be. The Remo and Amahuaca weren't just from another tributary, but from the eastern side of one. That is hundreds of kilometers away and separated by mountains and rivers from the existing missions and their own captive populations.

But none of this mattered. Not at all.

The missionaries were solely concerned with filling those missions. Like Pizarro, like Las Casas, they had been ordained by the same God to save souls. If it meant taming the people and the environment, that's what it took. People died. It happens.

Like Woodroffe, they were there to save lives. Only in this case, it was from eternal damnation.

They were there to extract a resource that had been left behind and discarded. Resources that they felt they were entitled to. Resources they deserved.

If they had been asked at the time, they'd probably say the same as Woodroffe: *for me and my family.*

At a glance, it's easy to grab on to any of these snapshots and succumb to the convenient story here: this is history. This is what happened. The natives had slaves. The natives had warfare. The missionaries, like Pizarro, like Woodroffe, just wanted to help. Those forests and mountains were just too damn valuable to let those resources waste away, unused. It's tragic and messy, but it is what it is.

That's a position that we don't get to take.

When we start to sift through the muddied waters,

we find our civilization and ourselves as the culprit in a chain reaction that spreads into our own times. Precious metals still flow out of Peru and they find their way into every electronic device that we use in our search to seek out the most accommodating ayahuasca-based spiritual retreat available to us as we reground ourselves into a mosaic of pillaged mindfulness.

Meanwhile, the societies defined and redefined on the frontier of our civilization continue to bleed out. Not in a metaphysical sense, but a literal one. As they try to maintain some semblance of community and continuity in their world, we strip mine and denude it. It is an insult to an ongoing injury for us to start dredging their "cultural memory" for some deeper meaning.

But in this portion of the story, the hardest part isn't just that Arévalo is still dead: it's that she lived at all.

Civilization has thrown literally everything at these societies. To undermine them. To mine them. To tear them apart and destroy them on a core level.

This is what we have done.

This is what we continue to do.

For all the messiness, the people of the Ucayali fought back.

They resisted.

They were fully unprepared for what the colonizers were going to introduce. How could they not be? There were minor precedents among the Inca for what a starving civilization looked like. But the Inca lacked the ideological and infrastructural ability to expand a nation-state. They raided. They traded. They pillaged and plundered, but they didn't stay. They didn't seek to undermine the cosmology of these groups, even though it would happen incidentally.

There was no precedent for how insidiously the European colonizers would play on the previously minimal cycles of war and raiding. How an unending hunger for slaves and minerals could bleed out populations that were already facing a genocidal reality.

As ugly as things were, as hideous as the fragments can look, they eventually started to stack up against the Europeans.

And they began to stack up together.

Back along the Ucayali River, those patterns of violently resisting the missionaries started to take root quickly. In that region, the missionaries and soldiers of empire started to make prolonged attempts at contact and conquest in the mid-1600s.

They were met with force.

In 1657, the Shipibo killed all the missionaries who had been attempting to establish a mission amongst them.[70]

During this same period, 1657-1659, the Cocama who had been settled at another mission began to shift greatly. They began to formalize the position of chiefs and consolidate their power. They had developed a fierce reputation for raiding on the Huallaga and Marañón Rivers, where the Conibo had been selling their slaves to *reducciones*. They had previously raided with the Shipibo regularly, but as the spread of diseases and contact with missions disrupted the chaos, the Cocama and Shipibo declared peace. But only with each other.

By 1659, the presence and influence of the Shipibo upon the Cocama began to rightfully frighten the missionaries at the Cocama mission. It reached a tipping point and the missionaries were forced to withdraw from the missions.[71]

The following year, the Shipibo and Cocama attack the Huallaga River mission.[72]

At the same time, Franciscans took a major stab at establishing missions among the Setebo: first in 1657 and again in 1661. Both times, the Setebo—assisted by the Shipibo—resisted, forcing the missions to be abandoned. In 1663, a mission was established among the Shipibo, but hostilities forced it to be abandoned five years later.[73]

It happens again and again. If you dig enough, you just keep finding these fragments.

1695, Conibo revolt against new missions and massacre their Spanish occupants. Three years later, facing punitive measures from encroaching Spanish, the Conibo joined with the Shipibo and Setebo to respond. This coordinated resistance largely kept missionaries out of the region until the 1740s.[74]

This didn't end the violence. The Cocama population continued in serious decline into the mid-seventeenth century, leaving the Shipibo to try to push further into the Central Ucayali where the Cocama had previously established a very strong presence. This also put the Shipibo back at odds with the Conibo, who were now traveling even further to Franciscan missions to try to get iron weapons. They promised the missionaries that these tools would allow them to seize another chunk of the Ucayali. But, more to the missionaries' liking, it would allow them to enslave the Shipibo.[75]

In 1760, a serious effort to establish missions in the Ucayali had taken root. The Shipibo and Setebo were close to each other, but at this point considered each other enemies. So much hostility had been brewing and was fostered by the clash of colonial reality and the mission situation that there was equal hostility spread toward and with the nearby Pano, Conibo, Remo, Amahuaca, and Chayaga missions.

After seven years of turning on each other from mission to mission, the pot had boiled over. A Shipibo man named Rungato, who had been considered an ally and friend of the missionaries, broke the tension. He instigated a peace between the societies that led to one of the largest uprisings in the region in 1767.

In an act of reconciliation, the banded societies destroyed the missions and massacred the missionaries.[76]

This is all just a glimpse.

This is what we have: the history of a region shifting and shifted by the presence of a civilization that had zero regard for any and all life. It is horrifically incomplete and in the following near two and a half centuries, the waves and floods are often endemically worse.

There is no happy picture here. There's no glamorous Oneness that's hidden just below the surface, no innate truth that kept everyone from going overboard. The reality is ugly. Despite periodic pacts and assistance to overthrow missions and wipe out the colonizers, the patterns of exploitation and abuse continue. The cycles of raiding and warfare continue into the last century.

This isn't a resolved story with a start date and end date. There are real hostilities here: ones that pre-date European contact, but are in no way, shape, or form untouched by it.

This is all a part of a living history.

These are pieces that help make up the foundation for the situation where Ginsberg and Burroughs would stumble upon a vine and sing the praises of it. Where they would put it on the map and, barely decades later, an entire tourism industry would open up around it. Completely resolved with a mythic vision of cultural memory just ripe with meaning and ready to be harvested.

This is the ugly baseline for the crossroad where Woodroffe stood. He was beside himself that Arévalo had these songs and just would not hand them over. He was there to save lives. He was there to help.

He was there so that *her* culture, *her* knowledge, could live on.

And it was him who pulled the trigger. Twice.

Arévalo died before him. In her daughter's arms: before her friends and family.

And for his actions, Woodroffe was lynched.

Pizarro, it turns out, was also murdered. It is said that his final act was to draw a cross on the ground with his own blood and pray. He, in the story he told, was there to help. For him and his family.

I don't know if he begged for his life. I don't know if he died with any dignity. I don't know if he did draw a cross as he bled out and if he prayed. I don't particularly care. I know his story enough that his narrative, the self-appointed hero's story, doesn't mean a fucking thing to me.

His narrative matters only because his narrative is the one that we still tell. That is a story with an end point. A story that is likely to end with a fitting conclusion: one that bleeds out in a self-reflective whimper that is more pathetic than convincing.

That pathology of civilization, the one that allows our cognitive dissonance to roam free, is linked to a finite world. The world Arévalo died in. The world Woodroffe thought he could save. The world Pizarro thought he discovered. The world Las Casas thought he could give salvation.

Our world.

At a certain point, infinite hunger collides with that finite reality. History will become another story, highlighted by a glut of rotting infrastructure and leaching industrial products and byproducts. We return to a world where cognitive dissonance too runs out of fuel. Ashes to ashes. Dust to dust.

I don't know if Pizarro begged for his life. But I do know that two days after Woodroffe killed Arévalo, that he did. I've seen the video. I've seen the pictures of his body. I saw him dragged through the dirt. The moments leading right up to his lynching are there, on the internet.

Same place where he found ayahuasca. Same place where I found him.

The videos are horrible quality. I was actually a little relieved about that.

I never needed to actually watch Woodroffe die to understand his place in this world. The part that he had played in the history of seeking the Amazon as a resource: as seeing something else to extract from it for the rest of the world.

He is neither alone nor unique in that regard. His body joins hundreds, if not thousands, of slain missionaries that died in the same forest trying to convert enslaved and slaving natives into workers. That is the same forest where Pizarro and his kind had turned massacre into a macabre sport. A forest where rubber barons wouldn't think twice about maiming and dismembering natives to force them to work harder at producing rubber. A forest where hundreds of thousands of native lives were taken, the remainder left to sort the ruins.

He never needed to be the worst of the bunch. In fact, to me, it's the fact that he wasn't that makes this story carry so much weight. For the rest of the world, Woodroffe becomes the focus because he was white. The colonizer. The victim.

But this should be Arévalo's story. Another part of a cultural memory Woodroffe stated he wanted to uphold, one that shouldn't require more violence to have been heard.

And because of his actions, her voice, her memories, her experiences, are gone. Buried.

I want this to be Arévalo's story. I want it to be her words.

As an individual, Woodroffe silenced Arévalo. In doing so, Woodroffe ensured that the story of the Amazon, the story of colonization, frontiers, expansion, and extraction—civilization by any other name—is her story.

Recurring Nightmares

What stands out here is the mimesis between the savagery attributed to the Indians by the colonists and the savagery perpetuated by the colonists in the name of what Julio César Arana called civilization, meaning business.
-Michael Taussig, *Shamanism, Colonialism, and the Wild Man*[77]

It is possible that there has been no greater force to reshape life in the Amazon than one of the most recent: the rubber boom.

Lasting from roughly 1870 to 1920, rubber barons tore open the unhealed wounds left at the point of contact. In every way, shape, and form, what followed was updated from the pillage and plunder of Pizarro solely in having added updated technologies: technologies more efficient in killing and more proficient in their hunger for resources.

The role that had been established by the Conibo in the slave trade was amplified. Trickle down civilization, if you will. For feeding the Europeans with slaves, the reward was access to more steel tools, from the "technological monopoly of the Europeans." The "brisk material flow" rode upon the current of colonizer pathology: "the Europeans were bestowing civilization on the Conibo while the Conibo were saving the savages."[78]

By 1870, a regular target of Conibo raiding, the Remo, were on the verge of extinction. With the newly founded colonial economy drying up, the end of the nineteenth century saw the middleman role as "lords of the Ucayali" shifting. The Conibo were reduced to a form of slavery themselves in service to the rubber boom: debt-peonage.

"But that," in the words of ethno-archaeologist Warren DeBoer, "is yet another sad story."[79]

That's quite the understatement.

It's also a story within which accounts of the Shipibo and Conibo become relatively absent.

"The Rubber Boom," writes Scott Wallace, "would have been to the western Amazon what the invasion of the U.S. Cavalry was to the High Plains and the Rockies."[80] Real time written accounts be damned, there's not a single portion of Amazonian life that wasn't touched by rubber.

Wallace continues:

> By the time the rubber industry collapsed on the eve of the First World War, the entire western rim of the Amazon had been thoroughly upended—entire tribes gone, others barely clinging to existence. As the twentieth century progressed, dozens of tribes disappeared altogether around the Amazon, many before their existence was

> *ever documented, victims of disease, massacres,*
> *or aggressive contacts by ranchers, loggers, oil*
> *companies, even missionaries who imperiled the*
> *lives of converts in order to "save" them.*[81]

Rubber: a thing that we sorely take for granted in our modernized landscapes.

In a world where so many of us own cars, bikes, and, well, anything with wheels or motors, rubber—particularly in the form of the tire—becomes seemingly innocuous. It's almost as if it isn't there until driving by an auto salvage lot, junk yard, or abused creek bed makes it apparent just how many of the wasted and barely eroding pieces of industrial hubris are actually floating around. However much we disregard its presence, rubber became a crucial and central part of the rapid industrialization and mechanization that the modern world is built upon. We tend to focus on tires, but there would be no gaskets, combustion engines, or belt-driven systems, and don't forget that electricity would be impossible without insulation for wiring.[82]

Columbus brought back rubber to Europe as a morbid curiosity. There had to be a use for it. They just hadn't found it yet. Hadn't "discovered" it.

Throughout Mesoamerican cultures, rubber had none of the meaning that industrialists would grant it. They made balls of it that were used in ritualistic games.[83] Almost three hundred years later, Columbus' ancestors figured out a need for that mysterious resource too.

In the meantime, those rubber balls had been a complete quandary for the Europeans.

To give an example as to how unique rubber was,

it's worth hearing how mesmerized and confused the Spanish were with the sight of something that could bounce. In 1535, Gonzalo Fernández de Oviedo y Valdés took a shot at describing the act of bouncing—a then non-existent concept for the Spaniards:

> *These balls jump much more than our hollow balls—by far—because even if they are only let slip from the hand to the ground, they rise much further than they started, and they make a jump, and then another and another, and many more, decreasing in height by itself, like hollow balls but more so.*[84]

Had rubber not intrinsically changed everything about civilization and the world it was thrust upon—particularly the violent processes by which it would conquer and exploit the world leading up to the ecological disasters of domestication that industrialism super-sized—the baffling response of Spain's elites to a bouncing rubber ball would be, frankly, pretty hilarious.

The fascination with rubber stayed relatively uneventful until the experiments really started. There were some in the 1740s, again in 1805. In the 1820s there was a slight rubber bubble. That one was ill-fated from the start. Natives in the Amazon had long been weatherproofing cloth by infusing it with rubber. Some of the colonists took note and rubberized their boots.

By the time those rubberized boots got back to the United States, the fad blew up quickly. And it was swallowed by impracticality just as fast. On paper, it sounded great, but without having learned to stabilize rubber, boots became brittle in winter and would melt in summer. To top it off, the smell was apparently awful. Needless to say, the idea hit a wall and—as would confound and confuse the learned of the time—simply bounced off it.

1833, a bankrupt Charles Goodyear becomes obsessed with rubber.

He ends up spending the rest of his life attempting to find some way to stabilize it. In a bit of foreshadowing, he was in and out of debtor's prison; he dragged his family through financial ruin, losing two of his own children in the process. An accidental success in stabilizing it might have been a curse of sorts for him, at least while he was alive. He had no idea how he had done it and a sample of the stabilized rubber found its way to Thomas Hancock back in the UK who became equally obsessed—though he had far better funding and equipment.

In his search, Hancock was able to recreate the accidentally stabilized rubber, dubbing the process "vulcanization." His British patent was given in 1844, only to be followed three weeks later by Goodyear getting a patent in the US for the product.[85]

However, neither really understood the process.

When Goodyear died in 1860, he was still drowning in debt to showcase a product that he never quite figured out—one that would rapidly change the world for the worst immediately after his death. It turns out, in the words of historian Charles Mann, that: "Nineteenth-century scientists found bouncing balls exactly as mystifying as sixteenth-century Spaniards."[86]

Unfortunately for the rest of us, the budding world of chemistry produced results. Not long after Goodyear's death, they figured vulcanization out.

They made a science of it and industry ate it up.

With vulcanization, rubber quickly became a commodity.

And a cheap one.

Rubber primarily comes from a latex sap from a tree in Central and Southern America and a vine in the Congo. All of which were conveniently growing on the frontiers of expanding European empires. Places where the habit of enslaving and abusing natives was already well established.[87]

Because of this, it was possible for Europeans to exploit rubber in endemically horrific ways.[88]

Everything that Las Casas spoke of, everything that Pizarro, Columbus, and Cortés did? All of that and more come back to the surface. In the Amazon and in the Congo, a newer, bleaker era of frontier extraction reanimates the corpse of the conquistador.

The phrase "crimes against humanity" barely covers it. But the situation was so awful that it is the rubber boom that led a British Foreign Officer—one sent to investigate the cruelty of the rubber frontier—Sir Roger Casement, to coin the phrase.[89]

While there are blanks about the Shipibo-Conibo, it's not hard to fill them in. Every society in the Amazon took this hit. Some are just much better documented than others. Where the pieces are being picked up again, in the wake of the burst rubber bubble, the similarities are tragically overwhelming.

The timing for the process of vulcanization was frightfully convenient. By the time the industry would enter the full-on boom period, it would be preceded by a massive drought that hit northeastern Brazil between 1877 and 1880. The impact of that drought cannot be overstated; it might have been responsible for as many as 200,000 deaths from starvation. Workers from Brazil flooded the Amazon in the wake of the declining sugar industry.[90] From one boom to another: between 1840 and 1900, the Amazon's rubber exports quadrupled every decade.

Half of that rubber went to the United States.[91]

The drought refugees flooded into an old frontier with a new resource to exploit. In the process they took part in forcing the natives of Colombia, Ecuador, and Peru into slavery and then a debt-peonage system, although both systems mostly just overlapped. Effectively the natives were "terrorized into wage labor they neither needed nor wanted."[92]

Terror was a crucial part of this whole economy.

It is impossible to tell this story without touching on Julio César Arana. In fact, I'm a bit relieved because he's the focal point for enough historical analysis elsewhere that I don't need to delve too much deeper on him here.

Arana was an early adapter to the rubber trade. He's not alone in this, but his astonishing rise in the industry is nothing short of catastrophic. Getting rich in rubber demanded a kind of shocking brutality. A brutality not only reminiscent of Pizarro, but of the same measure and depravity.

He started out by trading with Colombians, but his unrelenting terror—imposed upon the natives of the Putumayo River, particularly the Huitoto—quickly built his reputation and career. He would become the manager of the notorious Peruvian Amazon Company, but he was far more than that. He was a frontier conquistador. His ruthlessness wasn't just aimed at natives, but other traders.

By 1907, Arana would attain the grandiosity that Belguim's King Leopold II had claimed in the Congo for this region of the Amazon. For the lower Putumayo, Arana became "the state itself."[93]

What that looked like on the ground – I'm not sure there is a better term than terror. My response to it is beyond words. It's just a visceral disgust. A potent rage that colonization provokes, yet the English language offers no real verbalization for.

I have criticized the Biblical sense of Las Casas' matter-of-fact recounting of unrelenting atrocity. It's not that he wasn't outraged, it's not that he wasn't sickened: it's that as someone who fully believed in the Bible, utter decimation had a precedent. One that was ordained by the same God he served. He had a ceiling and a floor for bloodlust.

The original inhabitants of the Americas—the very people Las Casas met first as a colonizer himself, but then again as a chronicler of atrocities—didn't have that. There was no precedent. There was no equivalent.

It was just decimation. In every regard, beyond the world as they had known it: beyond the cosmos as they had understood them. Forgive them for their sins, but even the wars that native civilizations had weren't this.

If Las Casas could be Biblical, Casement was clerical in his accounts of the atrocities along the Putumayo. Just as they were when Casement was sent by Britain to investigate the Amazonian mirror of what was taking place in the Congo at the same time. Casement was sent by the British to follow up on Walter Hardenburg's accounts along the Putumayo River in Peru.

Hardenburg, however, was more impassioned.

You'll have to forgive me for paraphrasing him, but while it's necessary to know what Arana's reign looked like, I lack the accountant's demeanor. An overview is grotesque enough.

The enslaved natives were worked day and night, with the least amount of food possible. The company and its thugs raided their gardens to feast upon while they raped and tortured the women and children. The captives were flogged incessantly, often down to the bone and left with sores and open wounds all over their bodies. When the wounds became too severe, they were left to die. Their bodies left for the captors' dogs to eat. The living were mutilated, just wantonly disfigured— castration, ears, fingers, arms, legs. Tortured with fire, tortured with water. Crucified upside down. Houses, gardens, and stored crops were burned.

The children...

The elderly...

It goes on.[94] I just can't.

Casement's report backed up and verified Hardenburg's account. That's what ultimately did Arana in. In 1911, three years before the whole rubber bubble would implode, Arana was dethroned from the ruthless frontier kingdom he had built. When he died, he was broke. But death wouldn't come until 1952.[95]

Lest you think there is some kind of karmic force in the world, consider an 88-year-old Arana.

When you remove the cognitive dissonance that civilization requires, it's important to remember for a moment that all of us, each and every one of us, as human beings, were shaped by evolution to be a nomadic hunter-gatherer. That is our baseline. That is what every society contends with and domestication—in all of its forms—seeks to tear apart and reassemble.

The egalitarian nature of that primal anarchy runs through all of us.

Civilization, we are told, is an ethos. An accomplishment: the grand finale of evolutionary success.

They are right, of course. About the ethos part at least.

The ethos of civilization is what led Pizarro to the Amazon and then Woodroffe in his wake. To stir the cadaver of a bloated Leviathan, a reanimated corpse that somehow expands as it decays.

That ethos is simple: civilization at all costs. It is predatory by nature and needlessly cruel by practice. Had the goals of civilization meant anything, a single fucking thing, then Woodroffe wouldn't be following the footsteps of Pizarro, the footsteps of Arana, just to find some way to magically cure addiction and depression. Post-traumatic stress disorder.

I can't even call it irony. It's not ironic.

It's genocide.

Casement, in the end, wasn't too far off from Las Casas. Las Casas feared for the souls that hadn't been given a chance to be saved before being killed. Before they, like the Huitoto, were wantonly maimed, disfigured, tortured: terrorized.

Las Casas served God. Casement served the government.

In his assessment, the cruelty was unnecessary, but the principles, the economics, were sound. If the company paid the natives with more goods, then the natives would work. And work harder. They too could be properly civilized.[96]

For his work, the British would knight Casement.

Just in case the point about civilization's ethos was missed, it's worth following Casement a little further. He would quit his government position shortly after becoming Sir Roger Casement. Emboldened by reporting from Europe's colonies, he took up the cause of Irish independence. In trying to acquire arms for an uprising, he was caught and convicted of treason.

In the process, his diaries had exposed a damning factor: they talked about his sex life. And he was a homosexual. No amount of pleading, no amount of goodwill earned for his work would save him. His honors were stripped and he was hung to death.

That was in 1916.[97]

Two years after the rubber bubble had burst.

Thirty-six years before Arana died of old age.

Terror, as a practice, was never meant for public consumption. It was a weapon and one to be hidden.

Terror comes to play a crucial role for a very significant reason: the Indigenous reality of the rubber trade looked no different than it had under the enslavement of Pizarro and other earlier colonizers. While there were half-hearted questions about slavery in the era of conquest, a real sentiment against slavery was growing in the following centuries. By the time rubber hit, slavery—at least, in name—had largely fallen out of favor.

As an institution of civilization, slavery, as Stanley Diamond points out, "was the most direct and brutal form, the incarnation of imperialism." But, he continues, "Imperialism evolves, it is never self-liquidating."

As society modernizes, the narratives have to change, even when the economic reality doesn't. Or doesn't significantly. Slavery would often be replaced by mercantile colonialism, only to later be replaced by neo-colonialism.[98] Each time, the perceived distance between the source of power and its subjects is removed. Leaving a vacuum to be filled with the perception of choice.

Or at least it is filled with the narrative of choice.

That narrative, like all of the others, would come to hold a central role. The cosmopolitan European backers of the entire colonial endeavor had really developed a distaste for slavery. At least, theoretically speaking.

In reality, the whole of Europe, like the entirety of the civilized world, runs off of slavery. This is as true now as it was when Columbus thought he landed in India, when Cortés decided to conquer Mexico on his own, when Pizarro got his slave permits in the newly colonized Peru, and when eco-tourists take part in their ayahuasca healing retreats. Form can shift, but the function remains.

While the Amazon and its occupants were being literally torn apart, reformed, and sold, the same was happening in the Congo. There, Belgium's King Leopold II was personally dipping his hand into the world of rubber.

His legacy is monstrously horrific. Joseph Conrad's scathing picture of the frontier, *Heart of Darkness*, was based on Leopold's grotesquely violent expansion into the Congo. The novel had fictionalized characters in the story, but it has only come to be more appreciated as a literal example of the lunacy of the frontier. That is a place where emboldened conquistadors are empowered by a cannibalistic orgy of unchecked and uncheckable power. And it always has been.

For all the horror of Leopold's reign—which is harrowingly documented in E.D. Morel's *Red Rubber*[99]—the truth was covered by the international image consciously being cultivated at the time of Leopold as a humanitarian and philanthropist. As his rule in the Congo was unequivocally measured in disembodied hands, disfigured and beaten slaves, and dystopian frontier kingdoms, Leopold presented himself as an anti-slavery advocate.[100]

There's that cognitive dissonance again.

Like Pizarro, like Woodroffe, Leopold was there to do good.

He meant well.

The reality of it is that Europeans bought this obvious bullshit because it suited them. That's something we ought to be horrifically familiar with. Rubber becomes such a non-thing in our world. Even with synthetic versions, rubber is still cheap. It still saturates our society and keeps our electrified modernity running.

And, at its base, that rubber still comes from plantations. It comes from trees. It comes from vines.

We don't have to think about it, so we just don't. It's convenient. History brought us here. This is where *we* belong. This is what *me and my family* have earned.

Me and my family aren't Leopold, just as they aren't Pizarro. And just as I am not Woodroffe.

This is what we tell ourselves. This is what we have always told ourselves.

Yet the largest broker for the Amazonian boom? Peruvian Amazon Company. That's a British owned corporation. Fifteen years before Sir Roger Casement would enrage the British, well-intentioned Peruvian writers were writing about *correrías*, slave raids.

This isn't new. This isn't something different than what we've been over already.

Armed groups stormed native societies. The men who fought back were killed. Women and children were captured and sold as slaves. As the rubber boom intensified, even though ecocidal practices threatened both the trees and the forests, it was the lack of labor in a heavily depopulated forest world that kept slavery on the frontier.

In 1892, a Peruvian writer had already written a eulogy for the public conscience:

> *It is not strange then, that there exists the cruel procedure known with the name of* correrías, *which consists of surprising the habitations of some tribe and taking the members of it prisoner. These prisoners are taken to far territories and are dedicated to work...This catechization has the advantage that the individual soon obtains precise concepts of the importance that his personal work has in the commerce of civilized people. ... In our century, the procedure is cruel and wounds all the fibers of our sensibility; but one must recognize the powerful and rapid help that it lends to civilization.*[101]

You don't even need to read into it, it's all right there: *that it lends to civilization.*

This is where the narratives matter. This is why Pizarro's story, like Woodroffe's, matters. This is what we tell ourselves. This is how our intrusions are justified.

There is a line that runs through the Amazon. An infection that spreads from the Uto-Aztecans who began to expand the trade networks of a relatively short-lived civilization further out. A line that spreads as the Mayans tried to hold off the inevitable and feed their Leviathan. A wound reopened when Incan warriors spread into the neighboring societies to raid. Damages that shaped and then reshaped a much lesser raiding complex: one that may or may not have predated European colonization.

"European explorers," we are reminded, "only step into local history, they do not set it in motion."[102] Oh but how they amplify it. Literally add explosives to an already volatile situation.

That evolving shape of imperialism wavers from the enslaving butcher to the paternalistic caretaker. A mood swing befitting the advocates of a fierce and jealous God: one that is, not surprisingly, being preached equally by every one of the agents of imperialism: the colonizer, the missionary, and the manager.

And, as we saw with the Conibo, the slave catcher.

Turning a free people into slaves made them useful. Turning slaves into workers makes them civilized. It's all for the greater good. The echoes were there all along. Las Casas lamented at the souls he wasn't able to save. The *encomiendas* and *reducciones* were plantations approved by God's divine supervisors.

So when the brutality of rubber tapping becomes the day-to-day life—by force no less—of Indigenous peoples, it's just to teach them about the values of hard work. Lessons taught by men with arms. More importantly, men with armed guards.

Hardenburg, the one who rang the alarm about the enslavement and brutality of the Amazonian rubber boom, referred to the Peruvian Amazon Company regularly by the name bestowed upon it: the "civilizing company."

In his indictment of the company, he was sure to point out that the natives were being "defrauded, driven into slavery, ravished, tortured, and destroyed" under a "republican Government, in a Christianized country, at the behest of the agents of a great joint-stock company with headquarters in London."[103]

In the rebranding of colonialism, missionaries come to take a starring role. They preach the virtues of a Godly world, while bestowing the destined impoverishment of the capitalist economy.

This is no accident. It was never an accident.

Debt-peonage became the out. The cover.

It became the story that made slavery—by any other name—palatable.

A story that could cover for the fact that slavery had never actually disappeared.

The rubber boom is inseparable from a system of debt-peonage.

Even some of the most notorious explorers and barons weren't exempt from periods of debt-servitude. Rubber wasn't just a pinnacle of boom and bust; the peonage system actually made it almost a caricature of it.

On the one hand, you had ludicrous excesses.

The port towns of Iquitos in Peru, and Belém and Manaus in Brazil, for example, went from nondescript frontier towns to vestiges of European fancy and frontier reality in a quick period. Belém became the region's economic capitol. But Manaus, nearly a thousand miles inland, became the masterpiece of European decadence: hosting homage to the finest of worldly consumables.

Perhaps the biggest flop in Manaus was Teatro Amazonas, an opera house whose details were a melting pot of Europe's gluttony, with highlights imported from Paris to Glasgow and Venice. The streets were set to a modern grid structure. All boosted by the once state governor, Eduardo Ribeiro, who is best typified by his overly-stimulated death in one of the city's many brothels.[104]

When individuals embody those excesses, you get some grotesque characters. Ones that are truly deserving beneficiaries of Pizarro's bloody legacy.

Carlos Fitzcarrald is one such person.

He was a ruthless baron, if the qualifier is even necessary. The glut of the boom pushed barons to try anything. And with a captive workforce, there weren't many obstacles. Some barons went after another source of rubber, *Castilla elastica.* Castilla trees produced *caucho*, a lesser grade of rubber; they grew on steeper slopes and in cooler climates. The lack of quality was made up for by the quantity you could get from a single tree by removing any and all caution to make harsher cuts and bleed the trees dry. It wasn't uncommon to take the whole tree at once.

Not shockingly, *caucheiros*—*caucho* tappers—decimated the areas they worked. This encouraged moving quickly and rapidly expanding that frontier. None of which would be done if it were not for the slave labor of native populations.

Fitzcarrald was one of those tappers. He had one

encounter with the Mashco of western Amazonia that is particularly telling. For all the bloodlust that these tappers had, like the conquistadors that came before them, they were always well-armed and well-guarded. Upon encountering the Mashco, Fitzcarrald met with a Mashco "leader" who inquired about the arrows the tappers had brought. Fitzcarrald handed him a bullet from his Winchester.

After examining the bullet, the chief rubbed it against his own chest and was emboldened by the fact that the bullet—a very foreign weapon—did no damage to him. Then he took out his own arrow and stuck it in his own arm, seemingly indifferent to the pain and gloating in the sense that his weapon was clearly superior. The Mashco turned their backs on Fitzcarrald, feeling victorious.

No baron, no conquistador, would ever be content with that exchange.

Fitzcarrald was no different:

And indeed, half an hour later roughly one hundred Mashcos, including the recalcitrant chief, lay murdered, stretched out on the riverbank which to this day bears the name Playa Mashco in memory of that bloody episode.[105]

My blood boils.

If you want to get a sense of just how dramatic the rubber boom was to this entire region, it was events like this that would come to reshape entire societies. In this case, that is exactly what happened for the Mashco. In response to this massacre, they took to the forest, where they remain to this day: isolated by choice. They live as nomadic hunter-gatherers in a forest where their footprint is so small that it takes training to even be able to see signs that they still exist there.

Yet there they remain on the run from loggers, miners, narco-traffickers, and leftist paramilitaries. Now, just the same as it has always been. At least since the colonizers came.[106]

It's a conflicting kind of feeling. It is reassuring to know that they're still there, at times removed enough from the diseases of civilization to even see a population resurgence, but it is the very nature and cultural memory of colonization that has kept them living as refugees in their own home.

This is the crossroad of a world without time and history. This one event, less than a few hours' worth of interchange, forcing the shift of an entire culture towards an isolation that continues to be a matter of survival over a century later.

Against that reality, you have Fitzcarrald himself.

His origin stories vary, but a popular one is that he arrives on the edge of a future rubber empire as a fugitive. Even if it isn't true for him in particular, it's a fitting start for most who ended up in the rubber industry.

He started out in Iquitos as a rubber trader and dealer when he was twenty-six. It didn't take long for him to become, as many would call him, the Rubber King. He amassed a quick fortune built around moving fast. As a result, his children studied in Paris, he personally owned a number of natives under the old *encomienda* system, and his main house—built along the upper Ucayali—was the image of luxury, surrounded by gardens tended, in turn, by Chinese slaves.

He had a steamboat built to manage the complex

and dangerous rivers throughout the Amazon. On board, you had comfortable cabins and more luxury than the most honored of patrons could take in while sipping French wines.

Off the ship, the rowdy, entitled crew pillaged anything in sight. Women were abducted and raped, the natives' gardens were ransacked, and everything in between was destroyed.[107] That is all behavior befitting the grotesque realities of enslavement and obliteration that Fitzcarrald built his fortune upon.

All of this was carried out by men themselves working off debts and, not uncommonly, finding a way out of their own fugitive situations. Not many of them lived long; the frontier has always been harsh, even for the colonizers. Pillaging might be a career, but it isn't subsistence.

Fitzcarrald himself didn't even live to see the bubble burst. The Mashco massacre alone is enough to show that when he did die, in 1897, it was already too late. He and another prominent rubber trader, Vaca Diez, died when Fitzcarrald's infamous boat flipped while prospecting rubber along the Ucayali River.[108]

As happens often, we come full circle.

Fitzcarrald's drowned corpse typifies the rubber boom. It lasted thirty-five years before being crushed. It builds up, struggling with debt. The blood, sweat, and lives of the enslaved create a frenzy of short-lived opulence. In the timelessness that the Amazon embodies, it's such a short period to have had such prolonged and lasting impacts. But that's how it is.

The Mashco-Piro still live on the edges, actively building their lives around being neither seen nor heard. Like the entombed body of Pizarro, the wreckage of Fitzcarrald's steamer remains on display in Peru. Just like a chunk of the Ancash region of Peru still bears his name: the Carlos Fermín Fitzcarrald Province.

That is a province where over 90% of the population are Quechua speakers.[109]

Nearly all have had their lives shaped by European conquest, only to be reshaped by the rubber boom.

Cultural memory: shaped by the likes of Fitzcarrald.

Colonial reality: forever in his shadow.

If one hand was excess, the other was deficit.

History circles around again. It lives and breathes the same air. The cycles become so familiar that we cross the same paths over and over again.

Here, there's another Woodroffe.

Joseph Woodroffe, an Englishman, spent eight years trying to get into the rubber industry. In doing so, he incidentally emphasized the awkward role debt plays in the whole rubber economy. In a number of ways, he himself became "a living debt."[110] He starts out running a store in the small town of Nauta, Peru. Nauta runs along the Marañón River, not far from where the Ucayali River feeds into it, forming the Amazon River. Iquitos, an outpost of the rubber boom and where Sebastian Woodroffe would seek out ayahuasca healers just over a century later, wasn't too far down the Amazon.

There, Woodroffe—Joseph, this time—would begin to acquire many natives. He did this by buying their "debts."[111]

Here, we get more of a glimpse of the unbalanced and disproportionate nature of relationships that Amazonian societies had fostered with outsiders. While there had long been a well-established hierarchy of colonial allegiances—ones that meant to bring slave raiding natives closer into trade networks, while keeping plenty of other societies out there from which slaves were stolen. As we've seen, none of those allegiances were more than temporary. That was true for both sides.

Societies with more clearly defined hierarchies made better accomplices for expanding empires. Along the Ucayali, the Cocama and Conibo were chiefdoms – societies with more structure and more of an established pattern for organizing for labor or for war. Shipibo and Setebo, on the other hand, remained on more of a "tribe" level.[112]

The tragedy of history is that chiefdoms being better organized for war worked both for and against them.

In the case of frontier expansion, taking part in fur, slave, or resource trades, chiefdoms were early adapters. Often trade gave new tools for an old trade: steel tools, machetes, and, most notably, guns. There was no way to scale it, so the decimation that came along with new diseases just led to complete desolation, both of human societies and the wild world that we all live within.

But that organization and ability to mobilize also made chiefdoms more formidable opponents for colonizers. They were able to put up a better fight and often trained enough in the ways of war that, quite often, they won too. Almost all of the most successful endeavors to exile and conquer the attempted missions were led or joined by chiefdoms.

Chiefdoms, however, are typically larger societies.

Ones built around larger gardens and more sedentary village structures. Having more of an advantage in terms of warfare came at the cost of another ecological bind: warfare arises only when there is something to defend—gardens, surplus, hunting zones when game become overtaxed.

In short, that means that chiefdoms also have the most to lose.

Societies that are more nomadic have the advantage of mobility. When the colonizers came, most often they pushed further out of the frontier range. Like the Mashco Piro, sometimes that can be workable if you're resourceful enough.

In terms of a worldwide view, nomadic hunter-gatherers and semi-nomadic horticulturalists were able to avoid a disproportionately high amount of direct contact with expanding Leviathans simply by avoiding them. This is one reason why accounts of the Shipibo are far less common than those of chiefdoms that were better suited to link with the intruder's economy. Chiefdoms like the Campa or, further into the depths of the Amazon in Brazil, the Mundurucú.

Needless to say, colonizers were never fair players. They are narcissistic opportunists. I believe that in economic terms, they're entrepreneurs. Free range marketers.

The debt-peonage system, "the dominant mode of exchange in the rural Amazon," was more than an updated form of slavery.[113] It became a form of enslavement that had freed the slavers, not the slaves. No one is going to accuse slavers of being humanitarian, but slavery, as a system, is so bold that it never felt the need to demand an answer to questions about freedom and value. Slaves were property. Which means that slaves were owned, possessions.

Know that I cannot say this without typing with white knuckles and grinding my teeth: slavery requires investment. Not that slavers gave a shit about the health and well being of any of the enslaved, universally the conditions of slaves demonstrate that. Moving from enslavement to debt-peonage, however, removes any sense of responsibility or ownership. It allows for indefinite servitude.

How debt-peonage works is simple, in a grotesque way: you are forced into an economic situation and, within it, anything you are given—tools, food, clothing, machetes, guns—becomes a debt that you must pay. The catch: the person to whom you are indebted to determines the terms of your indebtedness.

It's like slavery, but you're working off a bill for a situation you didn't want and for items you never asked for. Basically, it's slavery with a slightly different name.

The debts, in reality, are not "obligations to be paid off—rather they are the lifeblood and connective tissue of Amazonian society, for the debt embodies and continues a social bond."[114]

Debt achieves what the missionaries sought: a path for acculturation. If you wanted to turn subsistence gardeners and farmers into poor people, if you sought to dump them into an economic world, you have to approach it how a missionary would. No one wants to be saved through salvation unless they are first lost. To see the light of God, you must first think it's something missing in your life.

That takes a lot of force. A lot of breaking.

Rubber tappers didn't have time for it. Breaking

spirits was a lot easier if you break social and ecological bonds first, so that is what they did. Upend everything in someone's life, destroy their society and remove them from the world that they know, suddenly they'll be too shocked and disturbed not to tear into the forest collecting rubber to pay off equipment forced onto them.

The reality is that debt-peonage forces an economic world on people without an economic worldview. If the world isn't just resources to use and plunder, what is the measure? As Michael Edward Stanfield asks in his history of the Amazonian rubber boom, "what was a metal axe worth to an Andoke, Bora, or Huitoto who had neither seen nor owned one?"[115]

The Mundurucú were no different than nearly any of the other Amazonian cultures dumped into this economy. They had no sense of numbers, they had no written language. They were forced to take "part in an economic system they could not fathom, so alien was it to their culture."[116] When barons, ones like Woodroffe, were acquiring natives, they did so because they had purchased their "debts" from the debtors.

In the economic narratives of civilization, we focus on modes of production. There's that line history draws back to hunter-gatherers again. A line that, we are told, shows how we have evolved from the realm of wild nature and learned to tame it. Honed our abilities to transfer matter into something usable. As if our millions of years of existence had meant nothing. As though our hundreds or, at the most, thousands of years of domestication hadn't just depraved us all more than it improved the lives of a very few.

In that narrative, debt-peonage turned the natives

from slaves to workers. From gardeners into laborers. Debt forced the economy into their lives, just as slavery had. It didn't give agency within the world of production; it ensured that natives remained a resource. Debt hovered over them to be bought, sold, and endured in the quest to maximize the extraction of the Amazon.

The rubber, in latex and timber, was pulled from the forests and sent through a series of shanty refineries before being dumped into the world market, mostly through ports like Iquitos.

As Stephen Bunker puts it, the exploitation of the Amazon, the sheer destruction and decimation of the forest, its peoples, and its once intact ecosystems was never just about production: it has always been a mode of extraction.[117]

It was the shit zone of a globalizing, industrial civilization.

It still is.

Debt is intangible, unless the exchange is between two settlers: entrepreneurs exchanging a resource. There was never a chance that the natives would work themselves out of servitude. That was never the point. It never has been.

To give some scope to it, it looked like a Campa man who had to spend two years of hard labor cutting down mahogany trees in the forest just to pay off a cheap shotgun. Only that situation didn't happen in the end of the nineteenth century. It didn't even happen during the rubber boom. It happened within the last fifty years.[118]

This isn't history. This is the extraction of life from a living world.

A glimpse of life on the endless frontier.

And it was in that world that Joseph Woodroffe, a shopkeeper of Nauta, started acquiring natives. In his words, "any labourers who cared to work for me...I would assume responsibility for their debts."[119] As Woodroffe would state it, that debt had a price tag; one he presumed was within reason.

But this was never an economic question: it was a political one.

Woodroffe, theoretically, had an out. There were, after all, a number of stories that mirrored Fitzcarrald's—already dead enough to be a legend for would-be barons. If you were a part of the colonial world, you could strike it rich, typically if you were merciless enough to only care about the well-being of your indentured servants long enough not to carry their debts beyond their usefulness. These were investments for future riches.

Woodroffe saw the promise as he headed off with fifty-eight enslaved men and fourteen women. Like Fitzcarrald, he went for the low hanging *caucho* fruit. His captives spent a year on an expedition cutting down entire trees to collect all of the sap, leaving nothing behind but broken ecologies and shattered memories buried in the exposed soils.

That year was a crucial period. As quick as the rubber industry took the Amazon and Congo, by sheer violent force, it was gone.

Let's step back for a moment.

In 1876, a British explorer and failure of a human, Henry Alexander Wickham enters the rubber story. He's not unlike many of the colonial characters, he was searching for a way to make his mark and reviled only for his less than noble means of doing it. It turns out that if you decimate a people and a region, you can be a hero of history. Undercut other capitalists and you become a villain.

At least that was the case regionally. In Brazil, a country in which rubber had decimated its Indigenous peoples and forests, Wickham is an awkward enemy. Before his death, his role in England had rebounded and, for it, he was knighted.

Before turning to rubber, Wickham's search for wealth had him all over the map. Literally. Manioc plantations in Brazil cost him the lives of his mother and sister. He tried his hand at tobacco in Australia and bananas in Honduras. In a bit of contemporary super-food/fuel foreshadowing, he failed to launch a coconut plantation off New Guinea.

His ticket to personal success was rubber.[120]

Years before, a British tree bootlegger named Clement Markham had set off into the Andes to collect seedlings for cinchona trees. The bark of cinchona trees was used to produce quinine, the only successful medication used to fight malaria, which expanding European empires had been struggling with on the frontier. Peru, Bolivia, and Ecuador kept their cinchona supplies close. It was a profitable business run by cutthroat capitalists who had as much of an ecological awareness as the rubber tappers. It didn't take long for them to have stripped so many cinchona trees of their bark that the trees were almost totally wiped out.

Markham got his foot in the door. The seedlings found their way to India where they were able to grow.[121] Seeing the writing on the wall, he saw the same future for rubber trees. At Markham's direction, Wickham saw a way out of his failing manioc venture. Using Confederate ex-pats that had flooded the Amazon, failing to build a post-Civil War haven, Wickham gathered 70,000 seeds and smuggled them to Britain, leaving his family behind in the process.[122]

In turn, those seeds found their way Sri Lanka, where they faltered with fungus. But it wasn't over. Dutch colonists pushed for Malaysia and Indonesia. In 1897, Sri Lanka and Malaysia hosted a thousand acres of rubber plantations. By 1912, that had grown to over 650,000 acres.[123]

The tide quickly shifted. Faced with competition, the Amazon and Congo rubber boom had quickly burst by 1914.

This is the backdrop of what would become Woodroffe's failed expedition. By the time they brought their haul back, the price had plummeted and his load wasn't sellable. The man he left to run his store in Nauta had run off, taking the money and remaining goods with him.

The debts he had incurred in building his involuntary work force now laid heavily upon him. The natives, logically, ran off. He found them within months working for another patron. Woodroffe argued with their new patron to shift the debts he still held associated with those natives and ended up striking a losing deal. He remained in debt. He took a position as an accountant with the Peruvian Amazon Company, but when his doomed haul finally sold, it was for considerably less than he could bear.[124]

In the process of having exploited the debt-peonage system, Woodroffe himself fell into it. "I personally became heavily in debt to my patrons," he wrote, "for an amount which would require months of patience and self-denial."

Woodroffe—Sebastian this time—made so many public statements that only became worse over time. His intent told one story, but the shady underside of it was a colonial reality that he was neither equipped to see or endure.

And for it, Arévalo was murdered.

I just can't get past it: *me and my family*. The entirety of the colonial frontier, the weight of civilization: it all comes out here. *They meant well.*

Joseph was no different.

After facing that "self-denial," he states it plainly: "I was now a victim of peonage; from this day on my life was a living hell."[125]

A living hell.

Because of his own fall from debt owner to peonage to the Peruvian Amazon Company, it's no shock that Woodroffe—Joseph again—quickly changed his feelings on the entire rubber industry. It's not shocking that his book on the matter, *The Upper Reaches of the Amazon*, becomes a lashing out against rubber and the atrocities it is built upon.

A living hell: two years before Woodroffe's book was published, Hardenburg had used the same phrase. Only his usage was noticeably different: "The region monopolized by this company is a living hell—a place where unbridled cruelty and its twin-brother, lust, run riot, with consequences too horrible to put down in writing."[126]

Objectively, yes, the entirety of the rubber boom had created a living hell. But for the same reasons Woodroffe had come to the region in the first place, he wasn't able to see beyond himself. Beyond his own role in the hell rubber created.

In the opening pages of his book, Joseph condemns the "deplorable conditions under which crude rubber is extracted to cater to our own tastes in comfort and luxury lead to ameliorated conditions for the rubber gatherers." Mind you, his expedition included fifty-eight men and fourteen women put under this exact condition by his command for the same purpose of rubber collecting.

But here's the real meat of it. If his book served as a warning, if the reader was left with disgust for the system, "then I shall feel that my eight years' stay in the Amazon, with its consequent sufferings—mental, moral, physical, and general—has not been wasted."[127]

Me and my family.

That book was published in 1914.

Had all of these events happened just a few years earlier, I can't imagine this is the book Woodroffe would have written. I can't even say that he would have written a book at all. This isn't to say he didn't have mental, physical, or general suffering. I'd imagine he was rife with moral quandary. But did it stop him? No.

What stopped him was that economics had failed him. The very same system that was put in place to justify the moral sufferings of a society enlightened enough to frown upon slavery, but starving for the luxury and comfort that slavery brings. *It had to be done.*

In that story, these weren't slaves: they were workers.

The fuck they were.

Debt-peonage is a lie. Not a lie that we have told the natives, but a lie that we tell ourselves. It is the lie that makes the globalized world turn and keeps production going. Move along, nothing to see here. Just development, maybe some hiccups along the way, but this is the path the world has taken. The path, we are told, that we chose.

The path, as it is sold to us, that keeps on improving.

But it doesn't. And by now, there's no excuse for us to say or think otherwise. That's what drove Woodroffe to Iquitos and beyond. This time I'm talking about Joseph and Sebastian. Extraction. That's all it was. That's all it ever will be. A cultural memory, a plant: does it matter which plant? Of course it doesn't. The realities behind each, the rampant differences between an economy of rubber exploitation and eco-tourism are unquestionable. But is eco-tourism better because it creates cardboard Indians for tourists to take their picture with and go on life-affirming, stomach-turning vision quests to fill the gaping pit of meaninglessness that civilization sold?

Let there be no mistake about this: the idea that there is a voluntary complicity in Arévalo, or any other native, working at something as crazy sounding as The Temple of the Way of Life, has always been used as justification for the presence and persistence of imperialist frontier economics.

But this isn't production. This isn't labor. These aren't volunteers here to share cultural memories.

These are people and an entire region reduced to a resource and extracted.

Bled dry. Literally.

This isn't a choice. It never has been. The Inca might have stolen and killed—even in a ritualistic display of cosmic power—but they didn't stay. They hit these societies and that hit hurt. The sheer weight of civilization and utter misery and deprivation that poured out of Europe as it infected the rest of the world – there is no end to it. No equivalent.

Neither was ever good. Neither would ever last, but the Inca never fully colonized the Amazon. Never told the occupants that they were there to help. Never spread NGOs and other liberal, humanitarian philanthropists—ones as genuine as King Leopold II—in to spread a fucking lie about why they were there and whom they were there for.

Woodroffe—Joseph this time—got to wash his hands clean. Woodroffe—Joseph and Sebastian—got to become victims of colonial realities.

A living hell.

For reasons that neither Woodroffe would ever understand, that is absolutely true.

Visions of Silent Despair

*To call "discovery" the first invasions of inhabited
lands by Europeans is an exercise in Eurocentric
power that already frames future narratives of the
event so described. Contact with the West is seen
as the foundation of historicity of different cultures. Once discovered by Europeans, the Other
finally enters the human world.*
-Michel-Rolph Trouillot, *Silencing the Past*[128]

Cultural memory: that is where this is all building up
to.

That's what Woodroffe was there for after all. How
he wound up in Peru. How he got funded to go learn.
Following up on all the things he read about on the internet.

Those old, ostensibly ancient, cultural memories
that the Shipibo were harboring, the ones Woodroffe
would learn and uphold. Maybe even save the world a
bit with. The ones that he claimed are "a far more valuable resource than all the trees, minerals, and oil in the

whole Amazon."

Yeah, those ones: that's the cultural memory he was after.

This is where we are. This is where the power of historical narratives becomes most apparent. At least it is for those of us willing to pay attention. Or for those, like the Shipibo, like Arévalo, who never had a choice in the matter.

History, the story that gets told, that grand narrative that feeds into the old ethos of civilization, becomes a choose-your-own-adventure for the colonizers. And for people like us: the colonizer's descendants. Understudies. We get to be removed enough that our active role looks passive. We're just the spectators in the stands. Our hands are clean too.

We get to be like Woodroffe, who claimed, "I care for people, and I want to help."

History has led us to this point. This is the path. This is the process.

Me and my family.

"Never before has a path been so clearly laid out for me."[129]

Woodroffe, once again, is on point. But not how he would have thought.

Cultural memory, as Woodroffe calls it, as we tend to treat it, becomes ahistorical. Ambiguous even. In the telling of the otherworldly role that ayahuasca shamanism comes to play, we can almost be left to believe that this cultural memory was gifted upon the Shipibo. Bestowed upon them, harbored by them.

Untouched. Pristine.

By this point, if it wasn't clear already, we should be aware that this is completely and utterly untrue.

Culture, to the degree it can be defined, is the sum of our interactions. How a group, a community, responds to each other and the world around them. It is only the civilized that can be so disconnected as to think that culture is stagnant. If it were, we simply wouldn't have lasted as long as we have as a species. As civilization has drastically destabilized the earth's climate, we are quickly headed into a new era of climatic chaos; a world that is simultaneously flooding and burning, where oceans are rising while soils are drying.

That world, this new era of instability, is what stagnancy looks like. It is the sum of the extractive, exploitive, and productionist mentality that domestication slowly pours into our lives. It becomes the basis of the pathology of civilization, civilization's ethos.

It also looks like the conquest in the Amazon. The blade, the plow, the Bible, and the bullet: all acting in unison, just as they were throughout the world. All to feed a handful of European civilizations—themselves an extension of the civilization born in Mesopotamia— entitled by a placeless God to travel a path that had never been so clearly laid out.

It takes history, it takes the stilling of time, to have the audacity to think that the impact of conquest and colonization hadn't shaped and reshaped cultures everywhere that it went. As a species, it is true that humans can be remarkably resilient. Perhaps even, as our circumstances would have it, to a fault. But when we pull back in the slightest bit, we're seeing the immediate consequences of colonization in the Americas—with or without direct interactions with the settlers—of anywhere from half to all of a society's population being killed off by diseases, starvation, and bloodshed. Entire societies gone. Entire societies forced to face loss that no cultural memory could explain.

A loss that few cultural memories could co-exist with.

This isn't to say that everything about any of these cultures was gone immediately. What it is saying is that the snapshots that we are seeing aren't inconsistent: they are changing. Morphing. Responding. Reacting.

That doesn't make them less of a cultural memory. But it means that whatever view there is of a culture based around this flattened history, this alternate story line where the catastrophic impact of contact is removed, is laughable. But it's also just tragic.

Reality is more complex than that. Not because it must be, but because the nature of the frontier created it that way. All other Amazonian societies had to respond to the arrival of Incan civilization, most likely the Mayans that predated them, and the Aztecs after. These are societies already in a degree of flux by the time European decimation swept through. Those were events fresh in the cultural memory when this wave struck.

Being societies that were still very much alive, in a place where the heresy of the present—the ability to isolate a moment from a living world, where the past and the present flow in and out of each other—does not exist, cultural memory doesn't begin and doesn't end. It grows. It lives.

So what is it that Woodroffe was after really?

He wanted Don Juan. It doesn't matter if he realized it or not. He wanted the authentic rendition of an inauthentic portrayal of a historic reality cast onto an ahistorical fantasy. He wanted the untouched spiritual world that he believed laid in the heart of a society, despite over five hundred years of living within the crisis that his own civilization, the still-expanding empire that spread from Mesopotamia and infects the world slowly, created and recreates.

The fantasy became an untapped resource: a hallucination of its very own.

What he was after potentially never existed. At least not how he saw it. But it is the search that matters. There was a resource; he was going to save it. Extract it for the benefit of the rest of the world. It was there just as the Indies were for Columbus. Just as a New World was there for Pizarro. Just as it would be once again for Arana. Just as Joseph Woodroffe saw it, just as it ensnared him into debt-peonage.

It came as gold. It came as slaves. It came as metals and guano. It came as rubber. It came as oil.

It comes as ayahuasca.

For Woodroffe, it was his white whale. That's what led him to Arévalo. She stood in his way. And for that, he killed her. And for that, he too was killed.

We come full circle.

A living history, paved with the dead.

Rubber reshaped life in the Amazon in absolutely horrific ways.

The distribution and even identities of tribes and chiefdoms were shaken in the wake of the rubber boom.[130] Along the Ucayali, the Setebo became "culturally extinct," the surviving members merging into the Shipibo communities. The once warring Shipibo and Conibo had become so decimated that intermarriage and outside pressure resulted in their unifying, hence the reference to Shipibo-Conibo.[131]

But the reaction to the fall of the rubber boom was as uneven as its impacts had been.

For the Jivaro and Shuar, the rubber trade brought a lot more settlers into the region along the river. That meant greater access to the *tsantsas*—shrunken head war trophies—for whites, a morbid fascination of theirs. The heads were bought with steel tools, particularly with guns. All of this greatly agitated and promoted war between the Achuar and Shuar. While the demand for heads kept the rubber collection slightly at bay, the economy of the head trade was amplified by an increased presence. When rubber dropped, the access to this economy dried up nearly completely.

With the external market and pressures removed, between 1910 and 1920 the Shuar and Achuar went from raiding for heads back to trading amongst each other. War ceded.[132]

For the Mundurucú in Brazil, rubber shifted everything.

Like the Jivaro, Mundurucú also had been taking heads in raids. The settlers and the global market they existed within couldn't get enough of them. The Mundurucú would trade the heads for steel tools, but by the beginning of the rubber boom, they had begun selling manioc flour and other forest goods to the settlers as well. They became fairly enmeshed. By the 1860s, large permanent settlements were established.[133]

When the boom hit, the men began to take part more heavily in slave raids to feed the beastly rubber empire, leaving the women behind to tend the gardens and sell their goods to the colonizers. The result was a massive shift in the value of the sexes within the Mundurucú.[134]

The role of the chiefs was undermined by the role of rubber traders. In the new reality that was being built, global economics became a formidable opponent to the way their societies were organized. The chief once handled production and trade, but now everything was being determined by the traders, who were in turn reliant on merchant houses, and, ultimately, on the global gatekeeper, the import-export firms.[135]

Though it wasn't immediate, assimilation was the end result.[136]

Missionaries hadn't had much luck settling amongst the Mundurucú, but the rubber boom opened up doors for them. In 1911, just a few years before the boom would collapse, Franciscans had begun to establish missions. But the collapse of the rubber boom didn't end the presence and reality of rubber in the Amazon, it just shifted it. By the 1920s, rubber was selling again—alongside hides from wild game—only this time it was to the missionaries who were brokering it.[137]

Along the Orinoco River in Venezuela, things looked different for the Yanomami. The peak seasonality for rubber tapping coincided with the peak time to harvest peach palm from older, more remote gardens. This pushed the more mobile of Yanomami further into the forests at the right time, in many ways saving them from the devastation of the boom.[138]

That, however, was far from a buffer.

The Yecuana, also along the Orinoco, became heavily involved in the boom by the 1860s.[139] They had already been trading with the colonizers, taking part in slave raids for some time. This gave them far more access to steel tools and guns, weapons they would end up using on the Yanomami, who began to acquire and raid for the tools themselves.

When rubber collapsed, whites left the region, drying up the steady supply of steel tools with them. Unlike the Achuar and Shuar, this vacuum instigated more warfare. This time, it was the Yanomami dominating with raids on the Yecuana.[140]

Much would be said about the Yanomami later, as the anthropologist and waste of life Napoleon Chagnon would trumpet their warring—warring he himself had helped instigate—as evidence of humanity's violent state of nature. This act becoming just another grand moment of applying a flattened history to justify civilization: ignoring endemic, genocidal loss in the process.

Beneath that is the same story we've seen here. It is contact that bolstered the Yecuana, playing them against the Yanomami. This was not without consequence. Steel tools make gardening faster and easier, which is probably a major reason why their introduction into the lives of the Yanomami had them turn away from the nomadic hunter-gatherer life it would appear they had lived up until the nineteenth century.[141]

And those increased raids on the Yecuana in the wake of rubber: "the Yanomami adopted many elements of Yecuana culture, notably canoe travel, fishing, and manioc cultivation."[142]

There's that ethos again.

But we aren't finished with rubber yet.

The bubble might have burst when the price of rubber tanked, but nothing was over. As has been said, a lot of rubber still comes from the same trees and vines today as it did when that Amazonian ball baffled inquisitive Europeans for centuries. In Brazil, one of the most profound failures came in the form of Henry Ford's laughable, though ecologically and socially devastating, attempt to create an American rubber city in the Amazon: Fordlandia.

The project and city was founded in 1928, fourteen years after Malaysian rubber had undercut the horrific trade in the Amazon and the Congo. Ford, ever the industrialist dreamer, thought he could turn rain forest into a plantation and fully Americanized city, complete with rubber production factories, and lure American workers in. It was never going to work. He certainly had the money to try anyway. But the idea wasn't far off in principle: reduce costs by farming rubber and reestablishing the Amazonian supply and production chain into one region.

Like everyone else rooted in stagnancy, it's just easy to forget that the ecology of a living world doesn't really care too much about your visions. The city was abandoned by 1934.[143]

When innovation doesn't work, sometimes the original idea just doesn't die out.

In 1942, Nelson Rockefeller, industrialist and champion of the missions, was urged by President Roosevelt to promote American interests in Peru. World War II had stripped the rubber supply and Roosevelt tried to act accordingly.

In kind, Rockefeller helped fund and build the Trans-Andean Highway, bisecting the Amazon forest and bringing a more convenient path of civilization through it.[144] That also means leaving more civilization in its wake, a new realm of frontier towns given more access to Indigenous groups left exposed by the highway and all its residue and destruction.

Just outside of the highway and more accessible areas, in the backwoods of the Amazon, for people like the Mundurucú, not only does rubber still thrive, so does the debt-peonage system.[145]

Of course it doesn't end there. It never does.

That's the thing about living history, it moves in cycles. So to really understand the impacts of the rubber boom, we have to go further back.

There are aspects of native approaches to trade that we might consider opportunistic.

The idea that you could trade with the same society you might go to war with or raid would seem either counterproductive or contrary. Of course, international politics don't make a lot more sense than this. The growing network of geopolitics ensures that nothing is as simple as deals between two nations. Or even more in the case of wars between two or more nations.

The way that natives had approached trade with Europeans, based on the way that trade had occurred with Andean societies before them, was pragmatic. The items of trade were typically still regional. Still a part of the world that all lived in. Scarcity wasn't necessarily unknown, but the nature of the tools and items being traded weren't as radically different as steel tools would prove to be.

It can feel like one of those unfortunate moments of history that such a pragmatic relationship with trade had prevailed for so long that it would flood into the visions of the Europeans. Visions capable of becoming distinct or even totally separated from the civilization that produced those tools.

But even that perception is pragmatic.

The selling point of technology has always been a

degree of magic.

Tools in the world of a hunter-gatherer, a gardener, or even a subsistence farmer are very tangible things. Made of stone, wood, bone, or pulled together from woven grasses, lashed with sinew, there was no mystery to their origin. The materials didn't just appear one day: they were there. If they weren't around all of the time, at least they were available seasonally. In a cultural and ecological way, they fully made sense. Their shaping took skill and knowledge, but this is one of the things that can turn them into cultural artifacts. Ideas about methods, experience and mistakes are passed down and shared.

A tool is made for the sole reason of being used. When it's no longer usable, is lost or discarded, then it is replicated. Maybe improved as seen fit, but they are practical things. Functional.

Technology is different. Technology is a system. Each part plays a role: each participant plays a part. There is a division of labor inherent to it, but the origins of technology lie in the organization of labor. Lewis Mumford hammers it in: "it is doubtful indeed whether non-human machines would have been pushed to their present perfection if the elementary lessons in machine-building had not first been made with malleable human units."[146]

In creating something otherworldly, machines and machined tools, cloth, and weapons, enmesh worlds. The story of the Amazon is a reminder of what the extraction of raw materials looks like, but none of us ever see it that way. So while the idea of manufactured goods appearing magical might strike those of us accustomed to them as ridiculous, it's worth bearing in mind that someone living outside the realm of the frontier in the Amazon probably has about as much understanding of what goes into and on within a smartphone as someone who has used them for the last decade or so. We don't have to pay attention, so we don't.

But knowing how to use it doesn't mean we understand it or what its production and use entails. So before anyone gets too caught up in judging, think of the baffled academics still trying to figure out the creation and purpose of ancient Egyptian and Mesoamerican pyramids. Meanwhile, you can run to the store in the middle of the night to buy a drone or electric toothbrush.

Regardless, the manufactured tools suddenly appearing in the forest were intrinsically different than any tool that had been experienced, made, or used prior. They came without context. Like they can appear to us when they're sitting on the shelves at Wal-Mart, they're now just there. A part of our world that now exists.

That almost mystical view of steel tools is pragmatic too. It is rooted in history.

Once steel tools began to flood into an area, it never took long for their use to spread quickly, through use, trade, and war. For most of the Amazon's occupants, those tools might have come decades, if not centuries, before a single European followed.

For all intents and purposes, steel tools became a resource independent of Europeans. Europeans just remained the most direct source for attaining the alien technologies.

Regardless of how they got there, the impact of steel tools was endemic. In their efficiency, they had been able to rapidly shift subsistence into an ecologically dismal situation. Manioc, for example, is far easier to work with steel tools than any thing that predates them. More manioc meant more reliance on gardens and an increased prevalence of manioc beer. Which led to more episodes of drunken violence, violence amplified again with steel tools—machetes and, eventually, guns.

Steel tools quickly become a resource like no other.[147]

They were finite, but, in bouts, they could be readily available. That missionaries had used them to lure people in never seemed to help. Missionaries are still baffled when Indigenous societies will enter the mission, play along to get the tools and foods, and then leave. It's that pragmatic ethos at play again, so unfamiliar to the thoroughly economic world that we all bolster.

The goods take on a life of their own.

There's nothing particularly Amazonian about this. Along the frontier of civilization, in every direction, every region, you get this separation between tools and other manufactured goods and the people who produce them.

Maybe there's just something to the story of it. Never have steel tools or manufactured goods been introduced into a region without being part of a massive, sprawling and often unseen network of colonial debris and bloodletting. This brings disease, this brings the murdering colonizing force, the axes and chainsaws of loggers, unhindered rape, relentless torture and execution, an inexplicable hunger for gold, a pathetically whimpering inability to subsist, and the prayers for a God that speaks of a nonsensical heaven, while leaving a living hell in their wake.

From a native perspective, if there is a silver lining, anything at all, then it has to be those tools.

And in many of these frontier zones, that's exactly the mythology that arose. This led to what anthropologists would end up calling "cargo cults." This is a particular kind of millenarian movement: a movement that contextualizes the arrival of something tangible, such as steel tools, within an apocalyptic scenario.

This, I could only imagine, is what it all must feel like. To have this new resource, one unlike any other, trickle into the region, then all of a sudden these European settlers arrive with them, and meanwhile, the diseases they carry and the murdering pathology they hold results in the loss of half or more of your community? How would that not be apocalyptic?

Fostered by the abysmal love of catastrophe that the Christians would preach, the visions of purpose make sense: that "the ancestors will return, or God, or some other liberating power, will appear, bringing all the goods the people desire, and ushering in a reign of eternal bliss."[148]

The understanding, prevalent throughout Melanesian societies at least, was that steel tools and manufactured goods were a gift from the ancestors. In some cases, a gift from the gods: a gift that was intercepted by Whites and was now being held from the intended recipients.[149]

With or without the goods, millenarians sought to make sense of what could only feel and look like end times, even for cultures without linear time. Within that cultural memory, even within the lifetimes of many, there had existed a culture—*their culture*—that held on to a time before the Europeans came. A memory that stretched before steel tools and had to account for their spread and the utter chaos and viciousness that came with them.

Cultural memories fostered by having witnessed half of a society dying because of disease and warfare. Cultural memories of seeing everyone die. Of seeing children torn from their mothers and smashed. Of generations of women being raped. Of men killed and survivors stolen. Of being torn apart from the world you had always known, the culture you were from, and relocated, mentally and physically.

Those aren't the memories that Woodroffe was after. That's not the harmonious world that ayahuasca would expose and clarify after the vomitus induction. That's not the story Don Juan, or whatever his Shipibo counterpart might be, would have told.

As it turns out, it is those memories, those events, which would turn ayahuasca into a widespread native "tradition." But Woodroffe didn't care. He didn't have to.

Conquest was never an event. Colonialism never ended. Cultural memory was responding to it because all stasis was gone. Killed off. Starved and left for dead. Those that survived had to make sense of the unthinkable horror that had befallen their world. The unthinkable horror that was still being played out.

For them, salvation was coming. Because, for them, it had to.[150]

Once the door to salvation opens, the potential for a supposed messiah to arrive skyrockets. More importantly, the likelihood that people will listen arrives.

Sure enough, that is exactly what contact would

bring to the Amazon.

In that earlier telling of native resistance to missions and settlements, there's a blank spot.

It's the early 1740s, and the settlers and missionaries suddenly start to back out of sections of the Amazon. This wasn't an accident; this wasn't just because of economics. There was an uprising, but not just any.

Quisopango was a settlement that sat on the upper Shimaqui River in the Gran Pajonal area of Peru. In 1733, the Campa living there had given food and shelter to Father La Marca. In 1736, Campa families from another part of the Gran Pajonal area had been resettled there by force.[151] Missionaries had started to pull other families into the town.

This made it a fitting setting for the arrival of Juan Santos Atahualpa. May 1742, Santos arrives in the region joined by a Piro man. At the time, he was probably around thirty and wearing a red *kushma*—a "sleeveless cotton tunic."[152]

While there's no confirmation of aspects of his origin stories, as is often befitting of a messiah of any form, some things are clearer than others. He was a Quechua man and he had come by river from Cuzco, the same city taken by Pizarro just over two hundred years prior. A common story is that he too was a fugitive, having fled after he "killed his master," who was a member of the Society of Jesus.[153]

There aren't many official documents of the time, but needless to say, even an earlier view of Santos cast him as "a lying, power-hungry, fugitive criminal."[154] He had been schooled in early age by Jesuits in Cuzco, by priests that evidently taunted him in ways that become incidentally prophetic: "Look here who belongs to the Kingdom of Peru; as there is no one else closer to the Inca of Peru, this one is on the verge of rising up with the Kingdom someday."[155]

Give it a few years, but they were right.

It would appear that the impression the Jesuits had left never sat well with Santos. He would head to Europe as a servant to a Jesuit priest, but it would seem that his hatred of the colonial situation predated all of that. As early as 1729, he had been trying to organize resistance to reclaim "the rights of Inca lineage."[156] Whatever he had done prior, the details are likely lost to history, but they are all less significant than what would come after his arrival in Gran Pajonal.

Santos spoke Asháninka, the language and name given to this particular Campa band living in this region and settlement. He observed their spiritual rites. While we will never know exactly what he had said, he was able to leave an impression upon the Asháninka that was hardly befitting of their existing cultural memory, one that left no room for leaders or organization behind a single person.

Whatever he did say though, it made an unbelievably massive impact.

Within days of his arrival, the natives abandoned not only Quisopango, but also all of the missions along the Perené, Mountain of Salt, Chanchamayo, and Ene. Santos had his message delivered quickly, but what was shocking was the way in which it was heeded: "The entire central jungle came, as if the signal had been silently awaited for years."[157]

Along with the Asháninka were Amuesha, Piro, Simirinche, Conibo, Shipibo, and Mochobo: societies that had been warring, particularly in the prior few centuries since Europeans infected the region. The uprising had begun.

Uprisings in this region had made the most of that pragmatic relationship between societies. The very relationship that permitted trade but was also completely comfortable with raiding and warfare had worked before. Alliances, often temporary, were used against Europeans and settlers. But this time was different.

Santos was Quechua. The rebels weren't just natives.

This was a turning point. And it caught attention. Father Santiago Vásquez de Caicedo, a notorious missionary, attempted to intervene quickly. The exchange did not go as he had planned:

> One afternoon in June 1742, the Franciscan arrived at the upper Shimá. In front of Santos's hut, the Indians formed a semicircle that soon closed around the missionary. Santos came out, said some prayers in Spanish and the creed in Latin, and then sent for food for the guest. A short time later the messiah explained his ideas. He had come to organize the kingdom with the help of his children: the Indians, the mestizos, and the blacks purchased with their money. He told the viceroy not to try to stop him "with four Spaniards…because…he would wring his and his son's necks like chickens."[158]

Santos was making waves. Two missionized Asháninka were sent along with the mayor of Sonomoro to follow up. They had confirmed the role that

Santos had attained amongst the rebels. And also that, as an Apu Inca, his rights to the kingdom of the Inca were legitimate. But there was nothing innately Incan or even native about his approach or worldview: he was the embodiment of the millenarian messiah. The lessons of the Jesuits took root. He wore a crucifix and "was a Christian, prayed every day, read the doctrine in a book, and preached to the Indians as the priests did."[159]

He was opposed to violence, but the image being conjured by missionaries was of a bloodthirsty renegade. Santos came to embody two centuries of the open warfare that the frontier had wrought, soaked equally in blood and Christian doctrines. Doctrines that preached words and worldviews that were completely at odds with the realities that the missionaries and missions actually created.

Most millennial movements are inclined to focus on that "cargo," things like steel tools. But in the aftermath and continually unfolding reality of conquest and colonization, it was the very words used by the settlers that had real appeal. The notion of religious redemption had appeal beyond the insurgent uprisings that had wiped out missions and settlers previously.

The uprising continued to spread. Santos' word came with it: Pizarro and the Spaniards had taken his kingdom. With God on their side, they would reclaim it.

Santos wanted to achieve this without bloodshed, but nowhere in the frontier was it going to happen that way. The Spanish built forts to try and contain it, but a decisive moment came when they built a fort in Quimirí to cut off the expansion of the rebellion. Within days, the rebels had the fort and its occupants held up. Santos had extended the offer of two truces to the fort's Captain, Fabricio Bártoli, who oversaw the battalion of eighty men under his command. Bártoli kept holding out on the truces, awaiting backup to take the rebels on.

At the end of the second truce, Bártoli and his men tried to escape at night, but were caught. "Not one man was spared."

Months later, the backup arrived. And, "From the other side of the river, they could see that the fort was occupied by the Asháninka rebels."[160]

From there, the rebellion had continued to grow. By 1752, the territories taken from the Campa, Amuesha, and Piro were reclaimed.[161] And as we know by now, attempts to missionize and otherwise intrude in the reclaimed region would return. But the rebellion awoke a new unified spirit, a new messiah complex had conjured a syncretic messiah: a new phantom to haunt the frontier's attempts at expansion.

For much of the region, long term attempts to regain control over the Asháninka, Piro, Amuesha, Mochobo, and some of the Conibo "would be a practically impossible task."[162] By 1756, the rebellion was considered over. But Santos was never caught. He became an enigma. Like the true messiah, his spirit would outlive his body.

In 1766, it was said that he "had disappeared in a cloud of smoke." But he wasn't gone. The Rungato uprising that was mentioned earlier? That took place the same year it was said that Santos had vanished into the ether. That uprising involved the Conibo, Setebo, and Shipibo. It became clear that "Santos's rebellion had given the jungle Indians a previously unknown unity and had awakened in them an ancient taste for freedom and independence."[163]

In terms of cultural memory, there's almost a romantic justice to it all.

The synergy of the gospel turned against the preachers. It's one thing to applaud the resistance, to be thankful that for nearly a century, the tension it had built upon had kept colonization from fully taking place. But that comfort is not ours. There is no comfort in a war zone.

And that is exactly what this is. The threat of colonization was persistent. That missionaries had failed to make prolonged settlements isn't a testament to the free spirit that roamed the forests in Santos' wake, but the endurance of emboldened societies to defend that region from their settlements. There's no comfort in that for us, because there is none for them.

This wasn't stasis. This wasn't a new normal. It was a reaction. An uprising against waves of colonization and decimation: an attempt to understand where the world had gone in terms of cultural memories, ones still vivid, others increasingly less relevant in a world that had become a frontier.

In that search, anything is of use.

Anything that can explain what was going on would be embraced.

And that's exactly what had happened. That's why a Jesuit-educated Quechua could have staying power with forest dwelling horticulturalists. What was happening to them had no cultural equivalent. Nothing in that cultural memory could make sense of it other than the gaping hole left by the absence of half the population or more who had been taken by disease, starved, carried off, torn from their arms, torn from their breasts, mutilated, or otherwise outright murdered by colonizers for the previous two hundred years.

There are questions about the romance of the story of Santos.

We know that resistance, amongst the natives of the Amazon in general, but the Asháninka in particular, had already had a long history prior to the arrival of the "Lord Inca." Clearly Santos' gospel had draw and an ability to unify, but "its allusions to the Inca empire was as alien to Asháninka political practice as the teachings of the Franciscans."[164]

The political aspects of Santos' message, being rooted in a rigid hierarchy and organized deployment, were as foreign as the Christian aspects. For social and cosmological reasons, this didn't make much sense. But we also know that the Asháninka had protested the religious order and beliefs that Santos preached.[165]

Perhaps it was the alliance itself that was a call back to a truly central element of genuine and deep-rooted indigenity: the pragmatic nature of the relationships to be had between groups and between each other.

More than anything, maybe the millenarianism wasn't just in the synchronism of Christian and Andean worlds with the cosmology of the forest dwellers, but in the ability to use them. Perhaps the messiah and/or the apocalypse wasn't an embracing of Christian-infused faith as much as it was a hope for a cataclysmic reset. A chance to be done with the Europeans and their bloody paths, clearly laid out before them.

The colonial experience became the unifier, presenting itself as a common enemy, "the cauldron of the colonial experience." Which made it possible to dream in "an imminent apocalyptic transformation that would result in a reversal of the Asháninkas' fortunes and the end of the oppressive rule of outsiders."[166]

The apocalyptic dream: the dream to end the nightmare.

Bártoli was killed when it was clear that his backup wasn't coming. He fled.

It didn't matter.

Backup would come, but much too late. When they saw that the battle had already been lost, seeing the Asháninka occupy the fort they had come to help retain—now that would have a been a good end to that story.

But it wasn't.

The century of resistance that surrounded the Santos uprising—resistance that came with or without Santos—ended for a reason. The backup, as we know by now, was the rubber boom. There was a precursor. Starting in the 1840s, agriculture was clearing the Amazonian forests and trying to take off with one crop or another: another thing to extract. Some, like coffee, equally mired in slavery.

Rubber brought the most violence.

For those that did fight against it, resistance was nearly impossible. Rubber became so pervasive, the networks of slave raiders and catchers had expanded so much that fleeing was no longer an option: "traders watched the rivers for tappers attempting escape. Punishment for attempted desertion was harsh, sometimes unspeakably brutal."[167]

The settlers revived the old system of slave raids and slave trades. For the "civilized Indians," the old economic tide pool now came attached to debt-peonage, forcing a new level of brutality and new weapons that pushed the slave raiding system further out.

It was traders like Fitzcarrald that realized a crucial aspect of slavery that had previously been practiced more than preached: "The rubber dealer had understood perfectly that the secret to having calm, submissive slaves lay in distancing them from their native land." Removed from everything that they know, "the Indians lost all interest in life."[168]

If they won't join you, beat them down until there is nothing left but sheer survival.

Fitzcarrald and others like him would continue to agitate tensions between groups and then arm each in waves to bolster the wars amongst them. The flood of decimation that the rubber trade had renewed, the unity that Santos offered couldn't withstand. But the hope for a savior, the hope for the catastrophic end of the frontier, stayed.

In the ultimate act of manipulation, the traders themselves took notice. By no means were they beyond using it to their advantage.

Of all the instances of this, one is particularly disturbing.

In 1897, the Franciscan priest Gabriel Sala was off to Gran Pajonal. There he spoke with an Asháninka man who told him about fighting between the Campa and the whites. He told Sala of an *Amachenga*—"a class of mythical saviors"—who had descended from heaven to help the Asháninka in their battle. Sala pushed more. It would appear that "one such Amachenga was none other than the rubber baron Carlos Fitzcarrald."[169]

And there it is. In the narrative that Fitzcarrald

told, he wasn't just there to help. Like Woodroffe, he was there to save lives.

They just had to help him to help themselves.

Surely there are others. A number of them have records left behind. Others echo like ghosts of history. Rest assured, there are probably far more whom history's authors never would encounter. Would-be saviors of societies wiped out by rubber traders.

Cultural memories: never to be written down for posterity's sake. Never to be salvaged.

By this point it should be apparent that the trend here is extraction, plain and simple, by any other name. That old ethos: civilization, at all costs.

The targets of civilization's ethos have always shifted since Columbus and his contemporaries stuck their first lance into the natives on their native soil. They came for the land and all it had to offer. He was content to die thinking that where he had gone was the Indies all along. Meanwhile, bodies became currency. At the hand of the colonizers, the land was mined and cleared. Missionaries went to war with cultural memories, leaving a blank slate for teaching the principles of work, in the form of slavery. Rubber hit reset and this time they did it all more violently, more efficiently.

But, in the civilizer's telling, it was always just. There were always reasons.

It was always for the good of civilization. If the natives didn't realize it, it's because they weren't civilized. Or they were less civilized after they fed Leviathan its slaves. Or they just hadn't realized the glory that could come through a bit of hard work. The kind of hard work demanded of debt-peonage and reinforced with a regime of sheer terror.

The natives, in the civilizer's narrative, failed to understand that the Europeans were here to help.

Or, at least, that they were there to help themselves and their families.

Or for Progress.

It doesn't matter. They had a number of reasons, but really it's one: *me and my family*.

It might look messy, but, they say, it had to be done.

Santos might have vanished into the air, but it's Fitzcarrald's bloated corpse that stays in my mind. The savior that would never come, drowned in the turbulent waters of the Ucayali. The elegant cabins of his ship—once the decadent hideaway from the absolute carnage of rape and pillage that terrorized all of those along the rivers it navigated—were now soaked and worthless. No longer were they guarded from the elements.

The rotting impasse of an unquenchable civilization: just floating lifelessly. All purpose drained from it. Just the shell of the colonizer, the frontier in flotilla form, stilled.

It's a fitting end for Fitzcarrald and his expedition.

But it was too late. His damage was done. A hundred bodies sprung in his place, each collecting disembodied hands, feet, limbs, and heads along the way. Scorching the earth, defleshing trees, poisoning the waters.

Fitzcarrald's waterlogged corpse was being absorbed into the world he sought to contain, to tame: to extract. And yet, deeper in the forest, he still gets to be the hero.

A savior.

A cultural memory.

Juan Santos, a millenarian messiah, had fostered Christian ideals in his revolt.

It didn't matter that he was unquestionably not European. The "cargo" of a cargo cult need not always be rooted in just being stuff, manufactured goods. It can be ideas. It can be ideals. And it certainly doesn't need to be European in origin.

Ayahuasca got us here: those varied brews made from a native vine.

Ayahuasca is also proof that "cargo" can even be a plant.

It is important to realize that the spirit of Santos, for the Asháninka in particular, might have been far more important than Santos and his mission. This is where it's beneficial to have this rotating relationship where ideas or trading are capable of shifting. This is how a Christianized Incan descendant could command Asháninka, who, by their nature, didn't give space for the authoritarian role that such a leader or messiah might fill.

In all likelihood, they just got what they wanted out of it and were willing to tolerate the rest.

Coming from a culture that seeks to flatten everything, it can be hard to see that kind of nuance. To really understand what their participation might have actually looked like. We make it our job to supplant their actual cultural memories with the history that we have written. The history that makes more sense alongside the Bible that Santos was capable of reading and reciting.

That kind of thinking—ours, not theirs—is what has led us to look at societies battling and embattled by an ongoing frontier and just act like everything is as it has been. As it must be.

That kind of thinking is capable of getting things very wrong.

Ayahuasca, as it turns out, is one of those things.

The Yagé Letters sparked a kind of cultural revolution.

Ayahuasca, in opening minds, also opened the imagination. For those who partook, it was exciting. It was, in their eyes, an authentic experience. Life changing. This, they believed, was *it*.

At that point, the point when ayahuasca fanfare starts to trickle into a globalizing civilization, it begins to take on a life of its own. A new narrative was taking off. That ends up looking like a key point in Jeremy Narby's *The Cosmic Serpent*: "[Ayahuasca] belongs to the indigenous people of Western Amazonia, who hold the keys to a way of knowing that they have practiced without interruption for at least five thousand years."[170]

Short of Ginsberg and Burroughs, maybe Terence McKenna to a degree, Narby's effort has been among the most popular variations of the ayahuasca and hallucinogen narrative that rise in the wake of *The Yagé Letters* and Castaneda.

The premise, however, is no more authentic than Don Juan. Five thousand years, a millennia: you start to see time frames attributed to the "ancient" use of ayahuasca in the region, but pinning down where that comes from is a lot more complicated. A lot of it is pretty clearly excited conjecture. For the work of Terence McKenna, that would account for most of it.

In peer-reviewed academia, the idea still managed to float by. There is a generalized idea that the widespread presence of ayahuasca usage is a sign that it must be ancient. Further, the "extensive range of ayahuasca preparations in the pharmacopoeias of different indigenous peoples throughout the Amazon region indicates that its use long predates first contact with Europeans."[171]

If it is, it must have been. Considering what we know of both the history of the Amazon and the constantly evolving sense of cultural memory within it, that's pretty shaky ground to stand on.

Dennis McKenna, Terence's brother, had authored or co-authored some of the most prominent sources for this trip of a factoid. But even he is more conservative in nature. In a 2016 article, he speculates that ayahuasca use "can be placed sometime between 500 BCE and 500 AD." An argument, he states clearly, that is based off of "ambiguous evidence."[172]

This was ambiguous evidence that had come from Plutarco Naranjo, an Ecuadorian doctor who would later become an ambassador. The five thousand year mark came from a 1986 paper of his that was built around evidence that was even more ambiguous. So much so that in later papers he wouldn't mention it again, hence the more conservative timeline of 500 BCE to 500 AD.[173]

As is often the case, theories piggyback other theories. The excitement that had flooded the pro-hallucinatory spirit bled over into the world of ethnobotanists like Richard Evans Schultes. Anthropologists like Michael Harner, who had studied most with the Jivaro, joined in the choir, along with Peter Furst. When the timeline was declared as a long-standing tradition, there was little reason to look further to identify when it began.

This is a common issue when it comes to the history of narcotics, and particularly hallucinogens. Those who come to research it, quite often, are there to preach their gospel too. Don Juan-inspired fanfare of peyote led to a projection of it, as a hallucinogen, far into the past. Again, without any kind of verification, it becomes completely overlooked that fresh peyote has little to no psychoactive properties.

For those living in a desert region where long distance running was commonplace, among both hunter-gatherers and horticulturalists, the medicinal qualities of it—from aiding in endurance and abating hunger to treating snake bites—would have given it considerable standing without the hallucinogenic properties. Properties amplified by drying the buttons in particular seasons and taking enough of them to induce hallucinations.[174]

Like peyote, the "alkaloid concentrations in ayahuasca beverages are several times greater than in the source plants from which they are prepared." Also like peyote, "the alkaloids' biosynthesis in the source plants may depend on the weather, the soil conditions, and the season."[175]

For peyote, like ayahuasca, the contention surrounds the fact that clearly the hallucinogenic aspects do become a thing. Clearly that is true. But to extrapolate that back into long standing traditions and, even worse, to presume that those hallucinogens were a—if not *the*—defining trait of a given society, is an asinine presumption.

And we know enough to say it's either a misrepresentation or a lie.

The explorer and botanist Richard Spruce is often credited with "discovering" ayahuasca in 1851. What that really means is that he gave the vine a taxonomic Latin name, *Banisteria caapí*.[176] A year later, in the northwestern Amazon, Spruce had taken part in an ayahuasca ceremony, taking some of the brew himself, among the Tukano.[177]

It's worth noting that the Tukano were heavily impacted by missionaries, particularly among the shamans. There existed a form of shamanic curing devoid of anything we've seen among many Indigenous societies. The trance aspect is gone. The shaman takes up an almost secular role as the conductor of ceremonies, often giving the ayahuasca to the patient instead of, as becomes the norm elsewhere, taking it themselves.[178]

Consider Schultes' claim, that ayahuasca "enters deeply into almost all aspects of the life of the peoples who take it to an extent reached by hardly any other hallucinogen."[179] For being so pervasive and thorough, the documentation of it is freakishly sparse. As someone who is skeptical, I'd say tellingly sparse.

For those who have dug into the history of ayahuasca in the Amazon, the generous time frame given to its induction into any Amazonian culture is far more conservative than Naranjo's: *within the last three hundred years*.[180]

I should take a moment to state that this was actually surprising to me.

Hallucinogens, after all, had a longer standing tradition in the region. Uto-Aztecans and Incans were prone to using *Datura*, a far more lethal native plant than *caapi*. For groups like the Huichol, who lived apart from the Mayans, but would be trading partners with, supply runners for, but also be raided and enslaved by them, peyote had likely taken on a role as a hallucinogen rather than just a medicinal prior to European conquest.

Other snuffs, such as the *Epene* that the Yanomami used, co-exist alongside ayahuasca.

But hallucinogenic plants exist nearly everywhere. That they would become used, typically in a post-conquest era, says nothing about the long term and ancestral use, by those same societies, of those same plants. It seems likely that civilizations, like the Maya, Aztec, and Inca, might have spread the cultural use of such hallucinogens in their wake. Or at least I would be prone to believe that the impact of warfare emanating from these civilizations would give reason for hunter-gatherers and horticulturalists to turn towards them.

This, however, doesn't seem to be the case.

At least it is not universally.

It might explain why the Tukano were using it, if that is where the brooding wave of an up-and-coming Amazonian habit was originating. But it would seem that more is to be said about how it spread than how it came into the picture originally.

While Schultes was willing to take Spruce's excitement alongside the contemporary spread of ayahuasca usage on its own, there were earlier accounts for ayahuasca usage. In 1737, the Jesuit Pablo Maroni mentions seeing ayahuasca being taken. 1768, the Jesuit Franz Xaver Veigl records an account of ayahuasca being taken again. While neither priest mentions where this happens, it is important to note that both instances were recorded in the missionary's *reducciones*.[181]

We return to the frontier missions. Those places where the constant amplification of raids meant bringing in displaced natives from further and further away.

Creating and fostering a world where displacement and relocation—when they didn't result in death, as they so often did—would leave an empty slate on which the missionaries could breed a fear of God. That is the kind of fear that might incentivize the natives to get to work, like the civilized would.

As we now know, the goal of conversion was rarely of much use. But the existence of the *reducciones* didn't need to be measured against their stated goals of conversion to realize that the true impact of their presence was in laying both natives and native cultures to waste.

And it is in these encampments where the natives would share knowledge and experience, anything that might make sense of the foreign world that had been imposed on them, so close to home that they could still sense all the recently deceased of their own cultures.

Places where their cultural memory still contained stories of the time before the colonizers had come.

From there, the spread of ayahuasca was slow.

By 1800, it had found its way up to the Ucayali River.[182]

That slow growth isn't what would shift the entire cosmology of the region—creating a ritualistic exploration that all grew in one direction, much like the *caapi* vine itself.

It was rubber, once again, that would amplify ayahuasca. Open the doors of perception: both external and internal.

For the cultural memory that Woodroffe wanted, this is where it takes root.

That is, in the world torn apart by the terror of rubber barons.

A colonized world. One that existing cultural

memories just couldn't make sense of.

Healing is a universal human condition.

The communal trance of nomadic hunter-gatherers becomes emblematic. Dancing, singing, touching, feeling, being vulnerable, being open, and laughing: all of these things are done together. By a society: as a group. Among hunter-gatherer societies, this is the norm.

It's such a formative feature of our primal anarchy that it never really goes away. But it does shift.

The cosmology of nomadic hunter-gatherers is rooted in direct, unmediated interaction with the world. If you aren't storing food in a granary or in gardens, then your day-to-day sustenance is tied to hunting, gathering, and scavenging. It is direct and always available.

In that world, a healer isn't a specialist.

Among the hunting and gathering Bushmen, when asked who was a healer, it wasn't uncommon to have half or more of adults claim that they were.[183] And there's no reason to think that wasn't the case. A healer might have some particular knowledge about medicinal plants, but mostly they took part in the act of being present, of touching: helping to absorb pain and discomfort, repelling it from the person or persons impacted.

The healing trance never quite fades.

Among horticulturalists, it's fairly common to find it. But settled life brings its own problems, problems that the healing of hunter-gatherers might be ill-equipped to handle. A garden needs more tending than a forest. The ecological balancing act that comes with mobility starts to get challenged; witchcraft and sorcery—a malicious kind of cosmic magic—arise. New problems need new answers.

And so the specialist arrives: the shaman.

A shaman is no priest. Whatever clout they might yield is as fragile as their performance. The self-preservation of a shaman can "constrain how cosmologies are elaborated and represented," but it's a performance-based position.[184] The shaman seeks to explain what is happening on this world by transcending it.[185]

That often looks like the shaman becoming the personification of the trance.

In that regard, it's easy to see why the idea of a very deeply native origin for ayahuasca shamanism would make sense. There are reflections of this kind of healing, many of which typically don't include any kind of hallucinogenic or narcotic substance.

But the role of the shaman has more to do with dealing with a world in flux than the kind of healing that happens in a world that is more stable. The demand to make cosmological sense of the realities of conquest and colonization, the brutality that came back into the Amazon with the rubber boom––there's a lot more weight put upon the shaman.

During the years and aftermath of decimation among the Yanomami, it wasn't uncommon to see the *Epene* habits of the shaman resulting in an almost permanent state of being high, of wrestling with that realm between the dead and the living.[186] It shouldn't be shocking then to recognize that the frequency of ayahuasca use amongst Indigenous cultures corresponds directly to the anguish that society is under.[187]

None of this universal: none of this just happens in

a vacuum.

There's no switch in a society where the shamans arrive and the healers disappear. While the catalyst for the ayahuasca ritual comes from outside society, these healing aspects don't go away, they become absorbed and incorporated into the rites.

This, incidentally, is the reason that we can say that the idea of millennia-old use of ayahuasca across the Amazon is not true. Like everything in this region, nothing spread evenly. Though shamanic curing practices, namely ayahuasca-based ones, would become widespread, it is crucial to understand that, in the words of anthropologist Peter Gow:

> *It evolved as a response to the specific colonial history of western Amazonia and is absent precisely from those few indigenous peoples who were buffered from the processes of colonial transformation caused by the spread of the rubber industry in the region.*[188]

Sure enough, that checks out.

In Ecuador, the Huaorani were subject to slave raids for the rubber industry. Forced to face industrial machinery and the death that came along with it, they ran.[189] Like other societies that sought to remain isolated, this is a choice they made, but was far from ideal. It would reshape their culture based around evasion. Though they were largely effective, you can't say they weren't affected.

But this also reduced their contact with outsiders, including other natives, considerably.

Although ayahuasca use is common amongst their

neighbors, the Huaorani have just about nothing to do with it. Shamans might drink it, but there are few, if any, shamans among them. A shaman, in their view, is always capable of being a sorcerer, which makes them suspicious. So to be a shaman is to inadvertently admit to potential guilt in the event of cosmic wrongdoing.[190]

The *caapi* vine is something that they are familiar with, but they only use it in extreme circumstances. One, to be exact. If a child is sick with *daicho* fever, on the verge of death, they will be given *mihi*, an ayahuasca drink.[191] If they survive, they are considered *mïnyï mëmpo*, a jaguar father. A shaman, more or less.

However, if they have had ayahuasca once, that's it. The change is permanent and nothing is needed to induce a trance state.[192]

It might be that the contentious history between societies is what kept the spread of ayahuasca from becoming universal throughout the Amazon. Over time, that spread has been happening.

In recent history, the Ese Eja, hunter-gatherers of Bolivia and Peru have seen their head-holding trance ritual replaced by an infusion of ayahuasca-based shamanism.[193] For the Matsigenka of Manu in the Peruvian Amazon, they had used *caapi* on its own for an untold period of time. It wasn't until the 1960s that they got word from Matsigenka of Urubamba to mix *caapi* with *Psychotria viridis*, which is one way that *caapi* becomes hallucinogenic.[194]

Add to this that a number of cultures have recent cultural memory of ayahuasca being introduced.[195] Consider the geographical range of societies that are now associated with ayahuasca use and how they are all using the Quechua term for a native vine.[196] Consider that the increasingly universalized ayahuasca rituals mirror Catholic Mass.[197]

So while there are aspects of ayahuasca shamanism that would make sense for horticulturalists, particularly horticulturalists long having been in a trading and raiding relationship with the Inca civilization and its descendants, it becomes clearer that this is only a piece of the picture. There is little question that this might be how ayahuasca, in some shape or form, enters the current Amazonian picture.

From there, it spreads as some degree of a synergistic mish-mash of cosmological devices to try and understand the reality that the *reducciones* created. But it spread very slowly. Knowing the rate of loss in these periods, it's hard to say how much that had really even caused the ritual to spread.

What we do begin to see is that the rubber boom and its aftermath create an entirely different picture. All of the sudden, this potentially slow growth of decades and centuries reaches nearly every edge of the Amazon, spread most quickly by rivers.

Particularly rivers that lead to hubs of the rubber boom.

Places like Iquitos.

It's one thing to say that the rubber boom spread ayahuasca shamanism as we now know it.

But it might be closer to the truth to say that the rubber boom created it.

Raimundo Irineu Serra, also known as Mestre Irineu, was a Brazilian rubber tapper. Irineu was born in 1890, in the middle of the rubber boom. His parents were both the descendants of slaves. As the story goes, his first encounter with ayahuasca, in the remote jungles of the Amazon, came in the 1920s.[198]

Irineu had grown up deeply religious. And as is prone to happen, his brushes with ayahuasca had only deepened that religiosity. Foreshadowing a little, his future followers would claim that his spirit teacher, Clara, introduced him to ayahuasca, which would shift his history and, incidentally, the Amazon's as well. Clara, for a budding religion, is a pretty lackluster sounding name for an origin story. For introducing Irineu to ayahuasca, or, as it is said, "the doctrine of the Daime," she got a bit of a promotion. Irineu's followers would call her the Virgin of the Immaculate Conception and the Queen of the Forest. Humble names.[199]

What Irineu would stumble upon and ultimately champion was neither new nor unique. It's what has been called "mestizo shamanism" or *vegetalismo*. It was the result of the "inevitable mixing of indigenous and dominator cultures in South America over time" resulting "in hybridities of ayahuasca use that continue to evolve through the forces of globalization."[200]

The boiling pot of colonialism—having turned natives into slaves and having imported Africans as slaves into a cauldron of frontier expansion—was creating new hybrid cultures. *Vegetalismo* is a fitting outlet for a world thrown together first in expansion and then with modernizing expansionism. Just like the *reducciones* and rubber camps created situations where the enslaved and enlisted tried to share paths to make sense of this new reality, here you had it on a larger urban scale.

This is where ayahuasca would enter the world stage: an urban-centered combination of deeply Catholic traditions, a brew of wild plants from the forest, and a dose of Indigenous healing rituals. All observed, consumed, and regurgitated by rubber tappers and the urban poor. Long before it would become the subject of eco-tourist healing retreats, you had Irineu and others like him in Brazil.

Irineu stays with us though.

In the 1930s, he would found Santo Daime: a hybrid church built around ayahuasca. There are others, certainly more before, exponentially more after, but Santo Daime is the oldest active variant. It is also the one that would later export itself out of the region and into other countries.

The tameness of the name might be a sign of the times. A nod to the descriptive, yet unimaginative names given to Catholic churches. So while it might sound better than something like the Temple of the Way of Light, just give it some time. After Mestre Irineu died, in 1971, the church would split in numerous directions. The faction that took the mantle of globalizing makes a lot more sense: the Eclectic Center of the Universal Flowing Light, CEFLURIS.[201]

There are aspects of *vegetalismo* that align with millenarian movements.

But there are also stark differences.

Millenarian and cargo movements are about a confrontation. The ideas and ideals of those movements are a combination of post-contact circumstances with the religion and organization of the colonizers. But they are based around a direct clash with that reality, even if that might take a number of different shapes. It can be armed resistance; it can be conscientious refusal to take part in the dominating system. It can be any number of methods or approaches built around invoking the apocalypse: to be rid of the colonizers and to return the land to the people, potentially with the goods the colonizers had used against them.

Vegetalismo, on the other hand, plays on the role of the shaman. In the sense that there is an Indigenous angle, this is decidedly a part of it. A priest, the religious vestige of more organized and hierarchical socio-religious orders, has an authority that the shaman never will. Just as the shaman plays a role in interfering with day-to-day affairs that most healers never will.

Priests dictate the will of God or gods or spirits. Shamans seek to transcend into the spirit world and appease them. It is the nature of religion, particularly the literate monotheisms, to see the will of God and/or gods as pre-ordained. You can pray, but that's about it.

Catholicism and Christianity have no platform for the kind of religious experience that ayahuasca offers. Ayahuasca shamanism, in practice, has more in common with the traditions of healing than those of preaching gospels. Unlike millenarian and cargo movements, *vegetalismo* seeks to explain and make sense of the world that civilization has created.

And historically speaking, it is a reaction to heal the colonial experience itself.[202]

That is how *vegetalismo* developed.

That is what it looked like for Irineu, the descendant of slaves; also unequivocally enmeshed in the backwaters of colonialism. To understand what it has become, what CEFLURIS would help make it, the creation of this cultural phenomenon in the mestizo world plays an important part. That was a religion created and practiced in Brazil. Practiced alongside Santo Daime, most notably, by two other churches: União do Vegetal (UDV) and Barquinha.[203]

While ayahuasca seems to have played a minor role in some native societies—potentially, if not likely—prior to contact, the rituals associated with ayahuasca shamanism are rooted in the mestizo world and its place in Amazonian cities.[204]

Mestizo, as a term and as a concept, tends to be rooted in a hierarchy of peoples; "whites," "mixed-blood people," and "natives." But it is too easy to get caught up in the racial aspect. That classification was devised by Jesuits and later imposed by Franciscans, but it is, for lack of a better concept, more about culture than race.[205]

And that culture is born of civilization's old ethos: the need to tame the "wild Indian." Civilization at all costs.

Mestizo culture is the outcome of generations of conquering and missionizing natives, attempting to breed the "native" out of them and salvage their bodies for civilization. Most often, in the service of the economy: as slaves, industrial workers, rubber tappers, loggers, and miners. Mestizo culture creates its own cultural memory in trying to separate itself from the Amazonian world it was cast from. In this narrative, "there was no notion of conquest in Amazonia."

Whites didn't conquer the natives, according to the narrative, they tamed them: most notably with manufactured goods. Whites carried civilization, but they "were ignorant of the potent love magic of these forest people and were seduced by Indian women."[206] No matter how the story of colonization and civilization is told, when you remove the malicious nature and reality of

116

conquest, the story sounds radically different.

Conquest, of course, did happen. Colonization not only came with it, it had never left.

But this is the legacy that comes from having drastically depopulated and ripped the cultures of natives apart, forced them into slavery and the overall brutality of frontier extractionism, and then indoctrinated them with the ethos of civilization through missionaries.

Recall what the slave raiding Conibo said of their neighboring societies as they were stolen, killed, and then traded for steel tools. They, like Pizarro, were civilizing.

Cultural memory: shattered and reassembled. Patched back together by missionaries. Reoriented by steel tools given for slave raids. Field tested by rubber barons. Forever tied to debt-peonage.

Forever changed by the frontier.

It's hard not to see the defeat. But the reality of extraction creates this world. That is a place where, for five centuries now, every society was played by the colonizer against the others. It's a game of cat and mouse. But in the end you realize that the game was fixed and both the cat and mouse were already trapped from the start.

Because in this categorization, this world crafted by the missionaries, the mestizo are another resource. One to be played against the natives. Ones that will never be "white." It has recast the occupants of the Amazon into a situation where the mestizo lies socially in-between.[207]

Neither here nor there, the mestizo rides the fence between two worlds as the imposed "socioeconomic system is woven into the physical landscape of western

Amazonia."[208]

Ayahuasca shamanism, *vegetalismo*, holds that middle ground. It doesn't seek to overturn the socio-economic system nor does it seek to face the reality of conquest that the mestizo narrative wants to deny. It just needs to make sense of this world. It needs to heal wounds and find, deep in the forest, some semblance of place that turns that middle of the road into a place of its own.

The forest, in this mythology, remains another resource: a place to extract meaning from, but never to fully return to. The brew comes from the forest to be consumed in the cities. Ayahuasca shamanism becomes "historical sorcery," one that "allows a return to the beginning of history."[209] So while the mestizo story doesn't want to include conquest, it can at least find a place for the mestizo in retelling the story.

A story that casts that middle ground into an eternal, living cosmology.

Ayahuasca shamanism flows from these places. It flows from these cities.

The ethnographers and early hallucinogen enthusiasts that put ayahuasca on the map knew about ayahuasca because of this mestizo reality. The story told about *vegetalismo* being brought out of the forest? That is what the urban shamans were telling. As living history, as an evolving cultural memory, why wouldn't that be the story?

If ayahuasca offered the path ahead, why wouldn't it have offered the path out of the forest?

The burst of newness and excitement was just taken as evidence. Just as the spread of ayahuasca led ethnographers and historians to believe that it meant its traditional usage was just there all along.

This happens even though evidence to the contrary is all around.

The patterns of ayahuasca shamanism mirror the paths taken in establishing the frontier. The native societies in the forest have little respect for shamans and shamanic power. For the Piro and Campa, they considered the really powerful shamans to be those from downriver. That is, they were looking downriver to the cities of Pucallpa and Iquitos.[210]

Places where Arévalo would end up working.

Places Woodroffe would find on the internet.

Cities defined by the rubber boom.

Woodroffe sought to extract a cultural memory: to find it, to make it his own and export it as a resource to help people back home.

It turns out that the cultural memory he sought *was* extraction.

What Becomes of the Broken

Empty and emptying, the logic of domestication,
with its demand to control everything, now shows
us the ruin of the civilization that ruins the rest.
-John Zerzan, *Future Primitive*[211]

The entirety of what I know about how Arévalo saw Woodroffe is this: she said no.

The history and reality of civilization is innately patriarchal. In that regard, there's a lot more that should be said about this: 'white man kills native woman.' It is far too common of an event.[212] It's so prevalent that we can't even call it an event, it's systemic: a plague that spreads far beyond the Amazon.

But in this particular case, I don't know how much of that was a factor in Woodroffe's decision to pull the trigger. Neither the first nor the second time he did it. There's a telling of this narrative in which Arévalo's son is said to have owed Woodroffe a considerable amount of money. I can't verify that, but ostensibly—if there's any truth to it at all—he had paid for some kind of aya-huasca shaman training and either wasn't satisfied or satiated. Or he was just out of his mind over-indulging a powerful hallucinogenic brew that he didn't understand.

I wasn't there. I can't say what it was.

But unlike much of the international, well-intended civilizing reactionaries, I tend to believe the natives know exactly what happened. And who had done it. And what it was over. That they were there and that being native doesn't preclude them from being able to identify a white tourist, particularly one who's gun was used to kill Arévalo and whose clothes bore residue from those gun shots.

There's a wanted poster that was made by the Ship-ibo for Woodroffe before he was lynched. I've seen it described in the media as "crude" and "primitive," as though that leads to enough confusion to have gotten the wrong guy.

But that flier? It's a color print out. Photos on it are taken from his social media sites. His last name is misspelled: Woodofre. But that's about it.[213] There is no question looking at this that they all knew what they saw and knew who they sought.

So when it is said that he killed her for refusing to give him her songs or treatment, especially considering the past and its current iterations in the Amazon, I have no reason to believe that this isn't the truth or extremely close to it.

Like the virus of patriarchy flowing in the veins of civilization, that entitlement is also systemic.

Woodroffe was just another tourist, another Gringo out to save himself and the world in the process. Pulling that trigger didn't make him unique, it just meant that it also made him a part of the murdering colonizers in addition to the extractionist adventurers.

Among the Shipibo-Conibo, those extractionist adventurers seem to have their own three categories: New Age spiritualists, stingy ones, and "*Buenos*" –literally, "good ones." But it is worth noting that of the good ones, "most of them are considered *drogadictos* ("drug addicts") because they like taking drugs and this is why they also like ayahuasca."[214]

But this isn't a universal role. It is important to remember that, for most Indigenous peoples, that concept of "tribe" was mostly one asserted by Europeans who battled them. It made it easier to categorize and determine a structure: to give the idea that a tribe was similar to a nation. Meaning that it had elected leadership that was capable of speaking on behalf of or in regards to the entire community. Almost always, this was a colonial fantasy at first.

That fantasy, however, often became reality through practice.

Missions and settlements, *encomiendas* and *reducciones*; they sought to outright destroy whatever elements of a culture existed that stood in the way of either eliminating, enslaving, or otherwise acculturating the remainders. We've seen that chaos. We've seen that bloodshed. We've seen the losses due to the spread—intentionally and unintentionally—of infectious diseases.

That is a practice the New Agers have capitalized on: presenting monolithic ideas about some fantastical Native American Spirituality or Shamanic Journeys. Other ideas like it that amount to a whimsical spit upon the graves of the dead while sealing the fate of the living. It's bullshit. Complete fabrication.

The reality is that while political and economic systems do begin to emerge within horticultural societies and sedentary hunter-gatherer cultures, it still isn't the same as anything we've succumbed to in nation-states. It's not until the kings come into the picture that a real sense of political might arises. And while you do have that role within societies like the Mayan, Incan, and Aztec, the collapse of the Maya says a lot: that power withers quickly when the food stops coming.

As a courtesy reminder, that's been true of every other civilization as well. And it will be equally true for ours.

The power of politics lies in the strength of infrastructure and the ability of elites to keep everyone else fed enough or threatened enough to stay in line.

So even though many of the Indigenous societies encountered here might have had chiefs, and chiefs are an early step on the stage of political power, to assume that they held full political sway is to misunderstand them completely. When ayahuasca eco-tourism whitewashes their trade and posts up flowery renditions of the relationship between centers and the Shipibo culture, or whichever culture is in that particular region, they tout the same kind of flattened and uniform pitch that colonizers have always used.

Effectively, it boils down to: "if this is a problem, then why is this person doing it?"

To be completely blunt, for a lot of the eco-tourists, that's probably a really convincing argument just because they will deal with a lot of mestizos. Who is Johnny America to second guess who is or isn't actually a representative of the faux-culture a retreat claims is working there?

What we've also seen, however, is that the reality on the ground in the frontier is far messier than any picture we are likely to paint of it. Considering there is no Shipibo-Conibo government, there is no penalty for when individuals from Shipibo-Conibo societies work the retreat centers. There are frustrations and there are strong disagreements about it, but at no point is the reality of a "post-colonial" Peru going to lie in the hands of whether or not some Shipibo-Conibo people work with *Rinkos*, a term given to the Gringos: foreigners.[215]

The reality is the same as it has been for the past five hundred years: once colonizers started plowing down the forest and its peoples to make way for the economy, the economy stayed. It had ups and downs, periods of pushing forward and periods of laying back. But it is undeniably a major factor in the shaping and reshaping of this region and its inhabitants that where there is a potential source of exportable resources, it will be used.

Be it steel tools, manufactured goods, or, in this case, cash, that reality has already been established. Not by the degree of participation or refusal, but by the insidious persistence of civilization to just keep coming back for more.

It is that colonial reality that ayahuasca shamanism is reacting to as well.

Ayahuasca can heal, according to the traditions, but it can't make you rich.

That is a firm mestizo lesson of history right there. Anything that can be extracted from the forest is, to an extent, just like the forest as both the natives and mestizos experience it. It brings sustenance, but it can also bring enslavement. You can sell things from it to whites, but you'll still be working for them. They, the whites, will still be the ones who profit.

There's the backhand of the Christians: to be human, you must work. Doesn't mean you'll get anywhere, but once you've toiled, maybe salvation sounds a lot more appealing. That's the lesson that the missions, as *encomiendas* and *reducciones*, sought to teach. A lesson burned into the cultural memory of those who survived it.

No matter how much some of the ayahuasca retreats might want to look authentically native, or even authentically mestizo, neither of those groups are the ones getting rich. It's a source of income, sure enough, but it's isolated in its nature. In the eyes of many, even that meager amount is unbearably costly to the culture at large.

Lest it be unclear, the primary motivation for ayahuasca shamanism is money or some other form of goods.[216] In every way that the ritual is uncharacteristic of Shipibo-Conibo culture, it is most apparent here. Unapologetically as well. In regards to the curing sessions, "the relationship between shaman and patient is characterized initially by aggressive demands for money."[217]

What traditional elements of the healing practices do exist, they go out the door as soon as whites and other eco-tourists show up. Shamanism, in a hallucination of the frontier world, becomes a source of income. It becomes a draw for tourists and other colonizers to pay up.

For all the talk of the mestizo ritual being authentically native, the only reason anyone would believe that is because they paid for it. They need to believe what they are experiencing or have experienced was as profound as they wanted it to be. And the only way it could be that innately shifting in terms of perception and cosmic alignment is if that presumption, echoed across the internet and in books that are, at best, a homage to the notion of a post-modern embrace of "traditionalism," goes unchecked.

It's easy to show that lineage. It's easy to undermine that myth if anyone is willing to pay attention.

But the reason that people don't is because so many of us, like Woodroffe, like the people Woodroffe wanted to heal—*him and his family*—are damaged themselves. Like an addict, he was looking for a fix.

This time, it was a fix to fix the fix.

It's possible that the choice of ayahuasca is most fitting here as the new cure-all super-drug. In analyzing its properties, two botanists stumble upon a chief characteristic of the brew: "the creation of great suggestibility."[218]

You see, ayahuasca usage does have a cultural memory. It is, in many ways, a cultural response to a situation. It is the nature of the extractionist, colonial ideology that cultural memory becomes a treasure map of sorts. Another thing to distill. Another truth to extract. Another world to see. A new white whale, a new glimpse of hope that El Dorado exists.

Ayahuasca becomes the new gold.

In the drastic retelling of the world, the one that lies at the heart of civilization from its inception, everything is a resource. Every resource has value.

Tear it down, pile it up, prepare it, ship it, inventory it, distill it into the international markets of a globalizing Leviathan: the sum is all parts. Pieces.

Fragments.

A world torn into shreds and reassembled according to the false hope of finally creating a civilization that sticks around for more than a thousand years. The false notion that our hubris will allow us to outlast our ruins. This time, we believe, we'll get it right.

In this story, ayahuasca is neutral. The rituals are a cultural memory, but one to be recorded, replayed, and replicated throughout the world. Ayahuasca is a vast pharmaceutical resource. The songs are just a part of its DNA to unlock. A spiritual key for economic scientists regardless of the context it is used under. Cultural memory could be rescued from its culture.

Woodroffe would help save us all.

At its core, this is the pure, unadulterated entitlement of the colonizer. In case I haven't driven that point home by now, this is the eternal frontier of civilization. The idea that we have a right to every single thing on this planet: we have earned it.

Potentially, we will use it better.

The Shipibo-Conibo, Maestra Arévalo herself, got some window dressing worthy of respect from Woodroffe, but it's a song and dance he never was going to understand. It was something much larger than himself. But, in the end, something he was very much an active part of as well. She saw what it was, she saw who he was. And she said no.

In the end, civilization will break you down. It will tear you into pieces and use every last one of them. When your unbroken spirit—that part that still beats, that blood that still boils, that love that still struggles— is all that is left, civilization will try to find a way to use

127

that too.

That is the core of extractionism.

That, dear reader, is ayahuasca.

For the most part, native encounters with missionaries could be exceptionally brutal.

In many cases, systems like *encomiendas* and *reducciones* are indistinguishable from any other plantation or work camp that existed at the same time, even in the same place. In the bloodshed that is the conquistador's frontier, the mission might offer some hope for relative protection. In light of limited options and unending warfare, it might not seem like the worst option.

The pragmatic nature of Indigenous relationships made it possible to settle down, even temporarily, to try and ride out the storm or to regroup and resist.

Some colonizers, tappers, and slavers were savvy enough to pick up on that. To use it.

Missionaries, on the other hand, have never been as understanding.

This shouldn't come as a surprise. Missionaries, in our world, tend to get let off the hook. Like Woodroffe, we believe they meant well. They could stand in the middle of the frontier and point to the excesses to justify the morality of their own mission. They might not save bodies, but hell be damned, they could try to save souls.

If you believe in the Christian God, I'd imagine that means something.

Like every single person on the planet prior to something shy of two thousand years ago, I don't. It turns out that every other Indigenous society missed the memo as well. Most, like we've seen here, weren't so happy with the messengers either.

Missionaries get a free pass from so many solely because the narrative works well for us. We need that hero. If colonization is too bloody and ugly, then here lies Las Casas, a tireless defender of God's people. Even if they are sure to suffer eternal damnation if they don't convert, minor footnote surely.

I refuse to let that be the case.[219]

Considering our brief run-through of events, or non-events, in terms of establishing long term missions, it can be easy to think that a couple months or years in one spot or another, often with very few converts, wouldn't have a lasting impact. In some instances, that might be true. But to neglect the reason why any of those missions did last, even just a few months or years, is unthinkable.

The frontier is a war zone. It is absolute devastation and assault, even if it's entirely one-sided.

Yet even in war, the battlefield can become a relic. A memory to haunt those who fought upon it, a cultural memory for those who lived around it, but with time, it recedes. It begins to pull back from our vantage point and becomes absorbed by the landscape. That is why nationalists enshrine them in historical events, place them in museums or plaster them with statues and plaques.

The memorial writes history into the landscape, tries to petrify a moment into a physical space so that it occupies a temporal one. Bite-sized piece of a narrative, meant to bring about a visceral sort of pride. It's the way that we can look to the "achievements" of civilization and feel that they are our own cultural memory, even when we know absolutely nothing about their inner workings and maybe a handful of talking points, if anything, on how they came to be.

The narrative is about what remains. How it justifies the present at the behest of the future.

We give missionaries a pass because we abuse the pedestal we have granted ourselves. It might have been unfortunate, it might have been messy, but the past is the past. Mine it at will; just pay it no mind outside of the current delegated boundaries.

Narratives reset that landscape. History creates boundaries. The story becomes limited by what we do and do not see. And that's what distinguishes missionaries in the frontier: they had a vision to replace the older visions with. They didn't just seek to wipe people out; they sought to wipe the culture out of the people.

And that is exactly what they did.

Nations and corporations have used missionaries for one specific reason: to whitewash colonialism. They call it acculturation, but there's a more accurate word: ethnocide. Ethnocide is the obliteration of cultures and it "results in the dissolution of the multiple into One."[220]

One world order, one ethos: civilization, at all costs.

That there are ranks and tiers—hierarchies by any other name—within that one civilization doesn't dent the ethos. In fact, it's kind of the point. If there isn't a hierarchy, it's harder to get people to look up the ladder: first to leaders, then to God.

Missionaries are there to eliminate any and all cultural memory that stands in the way. In 1610, an archdiocese in Lima, Peru was upset with the lack of conversions happening in the colonizing process. Too many killed, not enough saved from savagery to be turned over to the economic world. In response: "Official support grew quickly for a systematic and forceful initiative to solve the widespread problem of religious error and to continue the absorption of the Indians into Christendom."[221]

Systematic and forceful indeed.

At every step, missionaries seek to chronically justify a worldview that intrinsically makes no sense to those they seek to convert. How do you preach the importance of Jesus's supposed sacrifice to a people with no sense of historic time?[222] And to those same people who undoubtedly are living with a cultural memory of seeing so many lives needlessly and cruelly taken?

We've seen what it takes to break people to the economy. How much force is required, how much decimation it takes, what kind of ecological upheaval is required. But the missionaries are nothing if not petty. Any connection to a native identity was a potential link to the world of the forest. That is a world in which natives would regularly rise up and leave the missions, often leaving missionary corpses and ruins in their wake.

The goal, like Fitzcarrald and Arana saw in effective ways to dispossess the enslaved, was uprooting culture. This happens across the world. In the US and Canada, a "Residential Schooling" program became the place to corral stolen native children. To throw them together with natives from all across each colonized nation: in being thrown in with children of different language groups and customs, they were reduced to becoming a "race." The first step in that process was to remove all cultural identity: clothing, hair, food, place, and, of course, language.[223]

Just as it was in the Amazon, when the prevailing liberal attitudes forced an end to that kind of program,

131

the missionaries just ended up switching things around. In Canada, you had events like the 60's Scoop: the theft of native children and removal from their homes only to be adopted out to white families in Canada and America. An attempt to assimilate by just pretending the cultural memory was gone. That is a cultural memory that was created because the parents of the 60's Scoop children were former students of the Residential Schools.[224]

Elsewhere in the world, the Residential Schools remain the same. In India currently, there is a "mega-school"—one that holds 27,000 Indigenous children: extracted.[225] Another resource.

Back in the Amazon, the systematic process involved belittling and force. Anytime an element of native culture appeared, it was targeted for removal. Writing of the mission at Chichicastenango in Guatemala, Norman Lewis writes of the priest of the Church of Santo Tomás, who claimed:

> *the mission would not accept that the souls of these Indians had been saved. Nor would they be saved until every vestige of the customs linking them to a hopeless pre-Christian past—including their dances, music and dramatic entertainments –had been abolished.*[226]

Mr Fernley, the missionary in charge, acted accordingly. He would take the free clothing sent from First World nations—places like Goodwill and Salvation Army—and give it to Indigenous people with cash for their traditional clothing, which they had to give up on the spot. Then those clothes were sold to tourists.

Tourists who would, in turn, subconsciously not realize that "the symbols of old had been replaced by Disney ducks, mice and rabbits."[227]

It's not surprising then to realize that it was in "multi-ethnic missionary *reducciones* or rubber camps, where many minority groups suffered from identity problems."[228] It's also not surprising that this is where talking about ayahuasca amongst natives also spread.

For missionaries, a cosmology rooted in a living history, grounded in place, remained the greatest threat. The ability of healers to mend wounds—physical and emotional—undermined the religious order. The use of shamans to interpret reality made them the embodiment of heresy. Even the introduction of medicines, a practice still associated with missionaries, is in part a means to undermine the curative powers that healers and shamans had.[229] Abilities and knowledge that had little power against the particular brutality and endemic consequences of domestication-borne illness Europeans carried with them.[230]

In other words, not only were the people under attack, but their culture and the cultural memories used to make sense of the world at large were being annihilated. Trauma defines the domestication process.[231] In this great rupturing, it's possible to reshape people: to runt them in the process of finding and defining yourself in a world that makes sense. That is a backdrop of adolescence that becomes the central feature of life for adults actively engaging in an entire ecology of relationships with the world and with others.[232]

By robbing that cultural memory, the means to understand aren't just removed, but trauma is created. As a wild being, humans are no less faced by potentially awful aspects of existence than any other wild animal. That is often played up for effect among the civilized. Spectacularized in full cinematic vision in order to bore in a sociobiological vision where life in the wild is one of terror and domination. Predator and prey: constantly at war.

That isn't reality, not in the slightest. But it doesn't mean that the world, as a whole, is a perfectly peaceful place either. Shockingly for some, there is middle ground.

Bad things can happen. That is why we have healing. That is why we have community. That is why we have cultural memory. No one suffers alone. No one is forced to face the world on their own. That is one reason stories play such a crucial narrative in human communities. That is another reason narratives really do matter. We want that story. This is how we interpret the world.

But we don't suffer the catastrophic reality of the frontier alone.

Gay Bradshaw's work on PTSD and the impacts of systemic violence amongst wild animals is extraordinary. Male and female elephants, all what we might refer to as *survivors*, "exhibit symptoms consistent with PTSD, including inter- and intraspecific hyperaggression and killing, and infanticide." The same can be said of the species that is cast as an eternal villain, one said to be one of the most brutal of predators: pumas.[233]

And the same can most definitely be said of us.

For those of us who live in a culture that is all just reenacted rituals of domination, rituals tied to a globalized civilization that is necessarily placeless, even the idea of relocation seems benign. It is anything but.

If your life is based off of subsistence hunting, foraging, and gardening, then your world is absolutely tied to place. The losses that come alongside conquest and colonization, anywhere from half to all of a population killed or taken by disease and starvation: they resonate with the rate of loss among any other wild population. From elephants to rattlesnakes to humans, displacement kills.[234]

Sometimes surviving can be worse.

In a study of the survivors of Nazi concentration camps, William Niederland found what is called "survivor syndrome." Of which, a persistent aspect was "alterations of personal identity." The shattering of everything they had known, the loss of a culture, embodied in friends and family, is a kind of displacement that no animal can endure. Niederland found that while most "patients complained 'I am now a different person,' the most severely harmed stated simply 'I am not a person.'"[235]

Is that how the people of the Amazon felt? Is that how the Shipibo felt? How much did trauma amplify the warfare and raiding complexes that contact had unleashed? I don't know. All of the absences of the Shipibo from these stories reveal something darker: the waves of colonization, this persistent frontier: all these colonizers there for them and their families. All these agents of civilization out to save the poor savages: to save them with work, as labor, slaves, and spirit guides. All of them sought to remove their agency at every step. *All of them.*

You don't ask a resource how it feels.

We don't ask people reduced to becoming resources how they feel.

That's not how colonization works. That's not how civilizations function.

We transpose our story line onto theirs. That's why the Shipibo are freakishly absent from a story that is ultimately about them. We didn't care. We didn't stop to check in. Woodroffe didn't ask Arévalo how he could tell her story: he wanted her songs, her knowledge. Her cultural memory: there for him to extract and to make useful on the world stage.

She said no, so he killed her.

For me and my family.

We have been building up to cultural memory because it becomes the latest of many reasons or justifications told to appease the supposed moral quandary. One that was felt, ironically enough, by Woodroffe—Joseph this time, not Sebastian—one that he would never feel enough to actually give a damn about the consequences of.

Woodroffe—Sebastian this time—was there because ayahuasca was the key. It was the thing that he read about. The thing that would save people in his own life, in his own world from PTSD and addiction: it would open up a new layer to old wounds and let them see the light.

And here is the ultimate in irony.

Ayahuasca spread because it arose in the center of a systemic and forceful effort at genocide. When the people still lived, it simply turned to ethnocide. The goal was that the people would be assimilated. All cultural memories were targets. But it is the failing of the domesticators to completely rid native memories that allowed pieces of that cultural memory to remain.

The healer of the pre-contact native societies was

amplified into the role of the shaman. The healing trance and all that came with it would shift onto this role. The sense of loss, those pieces of culture and place that were stolen, the people that were raped, murdered, torn, dismembered, tortured, enslaved, exported, preached to, and, ultimately, left to survive in a world turned upside down, created trauma. This isn't post-traumatic stress disorder as we know it because there is no post- to that trauma.

The frontier is an open wound.

The most direct cause might shift, but the underlying damage still remains. This is the world of extraction. This is the world of civilization.

This is what "at all costs" looks like.

Cultural memory, the one Woodroffe sought, the one Narby claimed had been "practiced without interruption for at least five thousand years," does, in the end, include ayahuasca.

But there is no uninterrupted form: there is only interruption. Ayahuasca, as the Shipibo-Conibo use it, isn't a magical treatment for PTSD: it's a part of a cultural means of understanding the world civilization has forced upon them. And it plays a complex part at that.

That is the world of extraction.

That is the world as trauma.

It's hard to see past the entitlement.

Even if I try to push aside the killing, even if I try to push aside the history being replayed over and over again, I still can't get past it. When people talk about the curative powers of ayahuasca, what is the reference point? What is being sold is a colonial fantasy: one in which colonization is entirely absent. It might be possible that this reality is what set Woodroffe off.

In all reality, ayahuasca's allure makes more sense in the mestizo world than in the native one. The limbo of trying to make sense of an innately domesticated approach to the world that is completely at odds with the reality of believing the forests are behind us. That nagging emptiness: that gaping hole. There's a feeling that something is missing, but the entirety of our functioning civilized lives are dependent upon believing that things are better. So much invested in the idea that things are getting better.

That notion clashes violently with our reality. The world burns and we can feel the flame. A part of us is ready for that millenarian apocalypse too. The idea of the end tends to feel a lot closer and more comfortable than it does just to assess our situation, to look down and accept where it is that we, as individuals, as a civilization, have found ourselves and do something about it.

Because there are ugly truths to all of this: every step, every day, and every action. I'm writing this book at my home. I live in the Ozarks, a bit southeast of dead center Missouri. The middle of nowhere. Within the last seventy years, the area I lived in was a company town. That makes it just a slightly more forgiving variant of the debt-peonage trap.

Six hundred years ago, the reaches of the then-collapsing Cahokia Empire would have branched out this far. A hundred and fifty years ago, the road that serves as a property line was the northern branch of the Cherokee route of the Trail of Tears. On a map, that makes no sense. But I suppose that's part of the point. Civilization, at all costs.

The old ethos: if you can't beat them, beat them down.

The land is unrecognizable between now and then. In the Indian Trails State Forest, there are no trails, just a couple paths that are called traces. Perhaps that is a more fitting name considering the history. The living history, the cultural memory left in what soil might remain, was clear-cut. The land was mined. The forests, both National and State, were replanted with non-native Virginia Pine, left alone for future logging. You can sense that much more was going on here, and that remains in a wild spirit that will one day retake these woods. Erupting, in time, into feral forests.

All efforts to remove the coyotes haven't stopped their calls from filling the air nightly. Black bear and elk, once eradicated, very slowly are making a comeback. It's a desolate place, but the haunting absence of culture—human, animal, and forest—is at times nothing short of overwhelming.

This place, with all its remaining wildness and all of its absolutely clear scarring, is beyond metaphor. It is damaged, but it is still here. You can still feel it. The sky at night can be so alive that it stops you. There is, in that infinite and eternal sight, a feeling that perhaps there is a future.

But there is also that gnawing sense that something awful devastated this region. That's because it did. It still is. The impressive waters of the Ozarks, with some particularly amazing caves, are flooded with the heavy metals and residues of active mines. The silence can be broken by the deafening sound of military jets, always doing more runs when global geopolitical powers hit an impasse. Constant reminders.

If it hadn't been for the rubber boom, there would be no electricity to have produced the synthetic insulation used on the wiring in this house, the wiring in my computer, all of which carries on through pylons and power lines.

This is the globalized world that we live in.

This is the world that extraction built.

It is the embodiment of entitlement: that we deserve this. So much so that none of us really know where these wires go in full, nor necessarily how they got there. None of us are ready to grasp what it takes to keep the power on. That's what makes it possible to separate history from a living history, part of a living, interconnected world.

But we still know that living world is out there.

We yearn for it. We reach for something that feels like it. We seek to fill this hole.

So while I remain enraged by Woodroffe, for his thoughts and actions, for not realizing the role he was playing out in the history of civilization, I still get it. I know what he was doing. I get how it is that we can say and believe that he meant well.

And every single time that thought plays out, Arévalo is still dead.

Those aren't contradictory realities: they are the same one. The very same realities that you and I both live in. The one where I've written this book and the one where you've read it. I can understand why people are reaching out in desperation for something like ayahuasca—an answer, a solution. It's the same reason why people develop addictions that Woodroffe was hoping to one day cure. It's also the same reason that Arévalo said no.

Ayahuasca becomes the fantasy. The escape. The out.

Like Don Juan's teachings, it becomes just another part of the New Ager's arsenal. One meant to give some meaning and perspective to life: some authenticity, even though it is flagrantly inauthentic. Because the cultural memory that ayahuasca did attain within the Shipibo-Conibo is a part of that context, that reality.

New Age mysticism and whatever other variations of it that exist are vampires. They're looking to suck the cultures they leach off dry. If ayahuasca can be added to the grab bag of metaphysical and ontological well being, then it's theirs for the taking. Pencil it in between hot yoga and self-help seminars on grounding. Pay-to-play Oneness.

Consumption, by any other name.

For all the want of authenticity, the shamanic curing that Woodroffe sought—the rituals he thought he could just recite in a facsimile of ritualistic meaning—was considered a medicine. Something that was capable of being enacted and reenacted anywhere and with anyone willing to listen. Or, more realistically, anyone willing to pay.

It is the most telling sign of the depravity of life that civilization truly has to offer, that Woodroffe and the industries that lured him down to Peru in the first place, that we think a culture is defined by its possessions. That we believe the entirety of a culture and the embodiment of its memory could be distilled into a cathartic retreat.

This whole time we've been talking about extraction, but this is the most literal form.

And Woodroffe is not an anomaly.

Margo Thunderbird summed up the phenomenon in 1988, thirty years before Woodroffe and Arévalo would be killed:

> *They came for our land, for what grew or could be grown on it, for the resources in it, and for our clean air and pure water. They stole these things from us, and in the taking they also stole our free ways and the best of our leaders, killed in battle or assassinated. And now, after all that, they've come for the very last of our possessions; now they want our pride, our history, our spiritual traditions. They want to rewrite and re-make these things, to claim them for themselves. The lies and thefts just never end.*[236]

Forty years ago, Geary Hobson called out the "White Shaman" as a new agent of colonial imperialism.[237] The white poets who began to follow Ginsberg and Burroughs, Castaneda and McKenna, claiming themselves to be shamans.

Leslie Marmon Silko was equally on point about the White Shamans: in an "attempt to cast-off their Anglo-American values, their Anglo-American origins, they violate a fundamental belief held by the tribal people they desire to emulate: they deny the truth; they deny their history, their very origins." The poetry written under the guise of a presumed shamanic identity "is pathetic evidence that in more than two hundred years, Anglo-Americans have failed to create a satisfactory identity for themselves."[238]

Silko was dead on. She is still dead on. She attacked Gary Snyder for his ahistorical attempt to find the supposed grace of a Native American spiritual amalgam. One that gives meaning to life within the American Empire that the Empire never grants. The White Shaman, the New Age enthusiast, the "culture vulture," wants all of the supposed Wholeness and none of the history.

It's not hard to see why. Snyder, in Silko's words, leads in a "direction which avoids historical facts which are hard to swallow: namely, that at best, the Anglo-American is a guest on this continent; and at the worst, the United States of America is founded upon stolen land."[239]

Within that narrative, Hobson points out, is the old idea of the white savior. That old routine dusted off: that the colonizer is just here to help. If, as the story goes, the "last" of the "medicine men" was dying off—a contrite literary device—then the position was open for the white savior to step in. To extract cultural memory: to embody it.[240]

In Hobson's words, you had the White Shaman poets and mysticists of the 70s, but in the 80s and 90s you wind up with full-blown "Instant Indian Spirituality gurus."[241] "Plastic Medicine People." "Shake and Bake Shamans." There are no shortages of terms for variations of the same principle.

And yet the idea remains, *they mean well.*

This, in a backward notion, is supposed to be honoring traditions. This is a notion that is pure colonial entitlement, one that is still as bereft of history and place as any. Those seeking out this fantastical world of faux-indigeny aren't healing. They most definitely aren't shamans. They are consumers.

Lisa Aldred ties this to the post-modern fantasies

that come with a denial of history. In her account: "as products of the very consumer culture they seek to escape, these New Agers pursue spiritual meaning and cultural identification through acts of purchase."

She continues:

> *Ultimately, their search for spiritual and cultural meaning through material acquisition leaves them feeling unsatisfied. The community they seek is only imagined, a world conjured up by the promises of advertised products, but with no history, social relations, or contextualized culture that would make for a sense of real belonging. Meanwhile, their fetishization of Native American spirituality not only masks the social oppression of real Indian peoples but also perpetuates it.*[242]

The commercialization of cultures is inseparable from a drive to capitalize on the sacred. Or, at the very least, commodify the concept of the sacred. If that means creating a Disney-esque reflection of supposed native perceptions, then so be it.

But for the most part, this all happens, and never having to confront the historical and contemporary realities that actual Indigenous peoples face, it becomes second nature to indulge in a colonial fantasy: that one where the colonizer's hands are clean.

It's hard not to see this in Narby's words: *uninterrupted*. In those claims, echoed by Woodroffe, there is some lasting and sacred thing here that the Shipibo-Conibo, like other native societies, hold on to, but this isn't a decision that we get to make. This isn't a reality that those on the frontier get to decide when to turn on and off.

There is no choice. The frontier presents a myriad of narratives about where it comes from and whom it is there for, but none of those, ever, give a shit about the lives they dispossess in the process.

This is a reality that was never lost on the Shipibo-Conibo.

It wasn't the death of Arévalo that reminded them of this. It was the death of Woodroffe.

When the news of his death spread, the police swarmed in immediately. Becky Linares, of Victoria Garcia, didn't miss a beat: "Do you think a police officer has ever come to this remote place before? Never! But when this Canadian died this place was full of them." This is what a *Guardian* reporter heard when investigating the double homicide. Linares continues with the full support of the crowd that had gathered: "There had to be a death for this to happen, but it was not because of the grandmother who was murdered, but because of the *gringo*."[243]

There should be rage. There should be outrage.

I can't read these words without being overwhelmed by it. The world of extraction, in the retaliatory killing of a Canadian man, gets a brief glimpse. That these voices are heard is incidental. Had Woodroffe gotten away with it, it's probable that nearly all of us would have never known about any of it.

This story doesn't belong to Woodroffe, but it's nearly impossible to avoid him. He becomes another catalyst. Another agent of civilization.

This is Arévalo's story: the story of the Amazon.

The story of extraction.

And that makes it the story of civilization.

This is that truth. This is that confluence of history and pathological disconnect which define the decimation of the Amazon, like anywhere on the many frontiers of civilization and extraction, and decontextualized based on our own experience of the utter failings of domestication. In resting on a fatal and potentially cataclysmic crash course with reality, a place of living history and consequence, we create and recreate civilization on a daily basis.

Another villager didn't miss the point: "A foreigner can come and kill us, day after day, like dogs or cats, and nothing happens."[244]

Cultural memory: shaped and reshaped by extraction.

Just as it has been. Just as it is.

And, in the end, as it stands, it is two villagers who were arrested for the lynching of Woodroffe. On the internet, across the platforms, you can see Woodroffe's friends and defenders talk about their supposed savagery. Dirt on graves not yet filled. This isn't how the civilized handle things. Echoing the pathetic whimpering of the colonizer, they just fall back on old standbys: *he meant well.*

It was ugly, but it had to happen.

Those who don't have to care, those who don't have to face this reality: those who are unlikely to be gunned down outside their homes, die in their daughters' arms, or have to fight for their right to live on their own, they will judge.

They will spit on the grave of Arévalo by never having to acknowledge it. Never having to acknowledge the pit of history that she, and far too many like her, have had to fill.

Not this time.

Not them. Not their families.

Arévalo is dead, but her story, her life, cannot be.

I refuse to let that be the case.

I am a part of this civilization too. But I won't forget her. I won't forget the world that created this situation nor my own role within it. I don't embrace that past, but I accept it.

And because of that, I will keep fighting it.

Always.

So what of the ritual? What of the reason Woodroffe was there in the first place?

At the outset of this chapter, there is a question about what Arévalo thought of Woodroffe, the man who would come to murder her. I don't know. I will never know.

But, most likely, he was some degree of a joke: the *Rinko* who took everything too seriously. Seemingly a stingy one at that.

That cultural memory that he found on the internet and put so much faith into, the one he spent four years in Peru trying to learn about? It was also a bit of a show. A spectacular event for tourists. It could bring in a bit of money for some, but realistically, it was a job. A source of income.

He wanted authentic. He got an authentic tourist experience.

Among the Shipibo-Conibo themselves, the shamanic tradition still carries on. In many ways, the old healer tradition continues to be pervasive. The ayahuasca ritual is considerably different than the experience given at the retreats.

Here, it is the healer—*médico* among the Shipibo—who drinks the brew, not the patient. It is the job of the healer, the specialist, to take the medicine and to transcend the world of the living in order to see what is the cause of illness for the patient. So they can then confront that reality and heal.[245] This is a process that is shrouded in Shipibo concepts of good and evil.

A general consensus among the Shipibo is that the use of ayahuasca for healing and sorcery is a recent addition.[246] Not surprisingly, a Shipibo curing session recorded in 1861 included no hallucinogenic or narcotic drug.[247] Likewise, while shamans claim that information can be passed through plant spirits, knowledge is primarily coming from other shamans.[248]

Sorcery remains absent from the "modern" ayahuasca ritual, the one for Rinkos, but this was a central role in the earlier forms of forest-based healing practiced by shamans with or without ayahuasca. In the draw to shamanism as a vocation, the older shamans ridicule the younger ones for their "missing diet," their lack of an understanding and experience of the psychological battlefield that ayahuasca is intended to enter the shaman into.[249]

This becomes an older problem. Shamanism, as a means to interpret the changing world, can also become a gateway to it. Among the Jivaro, payment for shamans came in the form of those highly valued manufactured goods. Because of this, there was a glut of new shamans all "attempting to accumulate wealth in the form of 'white man's valuables.'"[250]

For the Shipibo, this creates a very real problem: "Many *medicos* are shifting their main occupation from curing patients or producing and countering sorcery to providing spectacular experiences for visitors from the West." As *medicos* serve as healers, the absence of help creates a void of health-care options and knowledge. Here, healing isn't referenced as "an esoteric or spiritual way but rather in a pragmatic sense of treating people who are suffering from more or less fatal problems.[251] In the retreats, Westerners have access to professional medical clinics. For everyone else, the *medico* is the professional.

Ayahuasca takes on a new role. In a spiritually-oriented usage, it becomes a substitute for "the former system of pragmatic curing: a system that was preserved, developed, and kept self-reproducing despite epidemics, conquest, missionary conditioning, and rubber slavery."[252] It becomes an adaptation within cultural memory.

Those healing aspects remain, most apparent in the fact that the native variation of ayahuasca use is without the entire spectacle of the retreat. More to the point, "among Shipibo medicos, there is almost no ritual present."[253]

The rules to be followed during the ritual, to the degree that there are any, are typically just the preference of the healer, but for the Shipibo that aren't used to dealing with outsiders, they rightfully get a solid laugh about all the faux-ritual that happens for "Northerners." From wearing all white, to being silent during the hallucinations and beyond—none of that matches what happens when it's just natives taking part.[254] Even the strict ideas about fasting and singing present in *vegetalismo* are considered laughable.[255]

The real mystical elements, the main holdovers of

longer-standing traditions of healing, are completely left out of the Gringo experience. The aspects that
Woodroffe might have been after? They were being
held from him, as they would any other Northerner.
For good reason, the Shipibo have realized the threat
of teaching the tourists every aspect of this living history. They are well aware of the history and reality of extraction, fearing, as they should, "the economic threat
apprentices may pose by carrying away Shipibo-based
knowledge and earning a lot of money on their own."[256]

Perhaps it's not so hard to figure out why Arévalo
said no after all.

There is no mystery here: for the tourists that ayahuasca brings, that extraction never quite fades. As
soon as Northerners create a mirage of authenticity
back home, then the cash flow stops. If Woodroffe was
successful, then those taking part in the economy of
spectacle were the ones who would be threatened.

Yet Woodroffe was speaking as though it was his
intent and his right to collect this knowledge and share
it. To extract that cultural memory. The presumption is
that this is somehow honoring the Shipibo culture. For
many reasons, that's despicably untrue.

The most obvious aspect being that Arévalo was
killed and by Woodroffe himself.

Beyond that, it is abundantly clear that ayahuasca
doesn't uphold Shipibo culture, it tears it apart and ac-
culturates it by benefiting some as individuals. It does
nothing for the culture other than to encapsulate an
idealized version in gift shops and museums for tourists. It gives some work for a small percentage of Shipibo to become living props for a cardboard narrative.

A narrative where the eco-tourists can say they all

meant well.

A narrative where those tourists aren't seen as who they really are: missionaries of a globalized neo-liberalism in a neo-colonial frontier.

It is the Shipibo who suffer for this. The money that does come back into the community is a new uneven resource, much like steel tools and manufactured goods. It creates disparity and makes it possible for the Northerners' pride in individualism to infect their society.

As of 2011, a few dozen Shipibo made a living off of ayahuasca. That's a tiny fraction of the 50,000 Shipibo who had nothing to do with the whole trade and industry. Meanwhile, Shipibo rites and rituals that are unrelated to ayahuasca fade.[257] Those *medicos* that still exist end up focusing on the tourists where they can earn incredibly larger amounts than if they work with other natives. Becoming so engaged with the secular world of ayahuasca tourism, the healers no longer take the claims and more mystical aspects of healing—the consequences of sorcery—seriously.[258]

Within this, you have the consequences of commodification. Ayahuasca becomes another in a long line of super-foods or super-medicines, capable of being a cure-all. Only, in the end, to become over-harvested, abused, and catastrophically wrecked in its consumption.

The echoes of that aren't hard to see. Rubber. Guano. Individuals turned into slaves. Forests. Every resource that civilization encounters becomes devoured until it is too late. Then we're off to find the next fix so that we never have to stop and realize that the same pattern repeats over and over again.

Already we're seeing that pattern play out. The *caapi* vine is becoming over-harvested. In many retreat-rich regions, it is so depleted that it has to be imported in, creating a cost barrier that ensures that other natives aren't able to afford its use for their own healing.[259]

There is precedent here.

In the same region, the Western "discovery" of quinoa as a super-food resulted in a tripling of its price between 2006 and 2013. This meant that the Andean peoples who rely on it could no longer afford the staple grain.[260]

In the United States, a hipster infatuation with white sage, such as bundles sold in Whole Foods or things even more absurd like the $40 "Witches' Starter Kit" sold at Sephora, tears at the old wounds of both cultural appropriation and cultural genocide. Here, hipsters are celebrating in a sterilized purchase of a sacred native medicinal while not understanding its ecological fragility or its cultural history.

A recent history in which governments and missionaries—insofar as you can distinguish them—had enforced brutal punishments for practicing their own spirituality, their own traditions.[261]

Back in the Amazon, things were no different. Evangelical missionaries among the Achuar had "virulent disapproval" of the use of ayahuasca in the missions.[262] Protestant missionaries chastised the Matsigenka's medical and religious practices as "Satanic."[263]

It is not our place, not now, not ever, to allow ourselves to forget that the traditions that we are so willing and able to just pick up, consume, and discard as we see fitting are traditions and part of a shifting cultural memory that Indigenous societies have fought and died for. They have existential meaning for us, if that. We cast our dissatisfaction and disappointment with our civilized existence into them and hope that the plastic cast pans out in our favor.

This is nothing short of the entitlement of the colonizer. Same old recipe, but with new packaging.

And it is in the often flippant disregard and ease with which Westerners turn these traditions into fads and trends—ones that are prone to a quick death—that makes it just that much worse. Like the stoned out hipster wearing an "Indian" headdress at an open air festival or the "squaw" and "warrior" Halloween costumes or the ridiculous Indian-based mascots and imagery for sports teams, it is in our sheer indifference to the actual costs of civilization—from the devastation left in the wake of our orgy of consumption to the reality of catastrophic climate shifts and mass extinctions—that the link from Woodroffe to Pizarro becomes most clear.

Never before has that path been laid out so clearly for me.

Commodification provides an easy out. It allows us to consume something wild, something we can see as ancestral without having to confront history or account for the depravity of civilized life that keeps leading us back into this tourist relationship with the wild, with any community living closer to their subsistence than we are.

It's a place to put our own fears and sense of displacement. But we haven't figured this out. We haven't solved the old problem of White Shamans and Instant Indian Spirituality guides. They aren't just persistently hanging around: they are rapidly growing. The Amazon faces its own brush with a wave of Plastic Medicine

Men and Women because of ayahuasca.[264]

That's the draw of the retreats, but it flows back to us too.

The internet is filled with all kinds of shamanism shams. The shaman becomes an ideal just completely removed from any reality. A Don Juan for a new you. There's a link I was sent, to a place called Shift Network. Their site boasts of a free online seminar on "shamanic journeying:" "Through the practice of shamanic journeying, you can consciously enter into parallel worlds of consciousness in which you can receive their accurate and helpful guidance on whatever life situations you face."

The recording is free, but have no fear, there's more. There's always more: "And you'll also hear about the launch of an exciting new virtual program where you can put these insights into practice!"[265]

Pay-to-play salvation. Operators are standing by.

I've seen posts from white people talking about how they might be a shaman because of this or that experience. As though it's something secretly lurking within you, like a disease. Maybe like small pox. Maybe like how rubber lay dormant in trees or taunting hundreds of years' worth of Europeans staring at a bouncing rubber ball.

The answer is no. Unequivocally.

A shaman isn't a position that's just open any more than urban Americans have some entitlement to the supposedly curative powers of ayahuasca. Neither of these things exists on their own. Neither is meant to be extracted from their context and still have meaning. Neither was ever meant to be taken out of that context. Nor were they intended to be written down, frozen in time and space, to become a blueprint for a spiritual Oneness.

And if there was a secret portal to another way of being, one that was somehow fulfilling in a way of peaceful co-existence that magically caused the world to make sense, then why the fuck isn't that how they're being used currently? Indigenous societies exist within a living history, as do we, even if we don't realize it. There is history here. There is a present that is cast and recast in the world of colonialism. The world of civilization.

What isn't extracted now, most likely civilization hasn't found a way to use it as a resource.

Yet.

And that is how ayahuasca enters the picture.

It's yet another of a long line of extracts to be pulled from the Amazon. That is, to pull more resources to help keep this overblown civilization floating for yet another day. Like the bloated body of Fitzcarrald, like the entombed remains of Pizarro, the corpse of civilization sits on display in plain sight. The dead reanimated over and over again by any piece of a living world that it could fit into its economy.

If Woodroffe had an ounce of experience instead of just more lofty goals of extraction and salvation, maybe when he went out to the frontier—like the bums, dropouts, and hippies before him—he might not have just recoiled in the face of colonization and doubled down on his idealized version of native life. The one he found on the internet.

The one he hoped to find after he arrived in Iquitos for the first time.

Instead, reality clashed with his ideals and he went

full-on colonizer. It was too easy because that is exactly what he was meant to do.

That, after all, is how this narrative works. That's the entitlement. That's how you can kill everything on a living planet and still get to be the victim. And the hero.

It's easy to judge and laugh about cargo cults and millenarians when they aren't familiar. We've grown up with nothing but manufactured goods. The magic of their presence and function is so lackluster for us that generations of fast-food and microwave dinner consumers can't even imagine the appeal of a steel pot.

But this is our cargo. This is the colonizer's dream: to take this world, to tear it up, to consume the pieces, reassemble them into our machinery and build a better future. To consume the world we feel entitled to. Yet the hope is that in the process we discover some meaning.

The colonizer wrecks the world while seeking to find a way to fill this gaping hole of meaninglessness that civilization and domestication require. The void in our lives where meaning should arise from community: where our presence in a living world becomes a lived ecology instead of another philosophy—one that has to compete with all these nice neat categories we've made for how we understand the world: social, economic, and political.

That's why it is the very society that believes it has become the embodiment of civilization's progress that can't find a way to plug the leak of misery reflected in a *decreasing* average life expectancy as addiction, depression, complications of a shit diet of hyper-processed foods, homicide, and suicide pick us off. One by one.

Woodroffe thought he could just switch the program.

If we just had that larger picture, then maybe we could get the right frame of mind to just sit back and take the misery that civilization unleashes upon us. Unleashes upon the world at large.

You have to presume that at some point it crossed his mind that he thought this is what the Shipibo had done. As though Arévalo had somehow mastered the frontier. If she could straddle the world of ayahuasca and the world of the living, a world plagued by a history Woodroffe wasn't seeing, and come out okay and wiser.

More whole: more complete.

He came to Peru to feel something.

He brought the gun with him. He purchased it ahead of time.

When that feeling just wasn't there, he felt the trigger.

So how did Arévalo see Woodroffe? It probably took no ayahuasca at all to see that he was broken. He just didn't know it yet.

And every time, Arévalo is still dead.

By now, my contrast of Woodroffe with Pizarro might be an irritation of sorts.

Woodroffe killed one person. For it, he too was murdered.

Pizarro, if we wanted to count, I'm not even sure there's a metric for doing it.

So allow me to make this clear, there is no direct equivalence between the two of them in terms of scale. The difference is clear. History will be split on whether to valorize or demonize Pizarro. Moderates may try to find some kind of middle ground where he can be upheld with a supposed critical eye, but we all know that this is bullshit. Or at least we all should know.

Pizarro, however he is cast, is an unquestionable force not only in the history of Peru, but in his role in reshaping the world as the West poured itself into the oceans and spread throughout the rest of the world. Infecting it, like the many diseases that the Europeans carried. The diseases that cleared the land ahead before swords, guns, and axes followed.

History, more than likely, will forget Woodroffe. Not even history. His story is downplayed and overlooked in real time. The internet that gave him an awareness of the Shipibo is the same place that has shown, over and over again, that someone like Woodroffe will forever remain the well-intentioned do-gooder. His story has already cast a massive shadow over Arévalo's.

That doesn't sit well for me. That will not sit okay with me.

In the grand scheme of things, two lives might seem relatively insignificant. It was one event that unfolded into two murders. Contrast that with Pizarro. It's immeasurable. But this situation, this reality, is the problem. If we focus too closely on two murders, we never see the big picture. And that blindness is something that we don't deserve to seek solace from.

The reality is that Pizarro didn't set all of this in motion. In terms of the destruction that would be systematically unleashed upon the Amazon, the genocidal reality forced upon those who lived there, Pizarro was a player in it all. One of many. Bloodthirsty and unrepentant, he was both on a scale that should be unthinkable, but we have the documentation and accounts to keep us from being coy about what really went on here.

But Pizarro wasn't a shipbuilder. He didn't cast his

swords. He didn't cast the iron and harvest everything necessary to manufacture muskets and gather gunpowder. For one person, the cast pattern of his bloodshed has few equivalents in size and depth. Yet he did absolutely none of this alone.

Pizarro was given a place on the world stage because the civilization he arose from was starving. He rode in the wake of Columbus. He climbed the ranks as a murderer and organizer of the grotesque decimation of peoples under Balboa.

There is no context for Pizarro that absolves or forgives him. None. He deserves no context to make it seem like any of it was okay. But at no point was he alone. At no point was he ever the anomaly that his financiers and backers had to throw under the bus or turn a blind eye on. He was no mere cog in the machine, but he was still a piece of it.

He was a part of the unending growth of civilization. He still is.

In history, he has a place. But the same entitled, conquering pathology that justified his bloodlust filters into our time. It is, after all, the same world. We are complicit in the same civilization as he was. That is the same civilization that Woodroffe came from.

And it is the same civilization that shaped the world that Arévalo was born into and, ultimately, was murdered within.

We can forget Woodroffe because he is one person. One murderer. One murdered.

What could it matter, after all?

He meant well.

That excuse is just that: an excuse.

Forgetting Woodroffe isn't our place. It's not our

decision. Forgetting is forgiving. It doesn't just mean that Woodroffe will be redeemed. Not by those who never hear his name: those who never see his face. It ensures that this situation will happen again. Just as it had before.

Our history is fragmented. Our world is pieces stitched together in a colonial web of maps drawn and redrawn. Torn again by warring states, expanding empires, and corporations, then mixed and matched to meet geopolitical interests, often competing ones at that. It functions because we don't see the string that ties Pizarro to Woodroffe.

The same tie that holds the Shipibo-Conibo to the wars of the Inca, the wrath of Pizarro, centuries of the slave trade, the agrarian and industrial nightmares that slavery fed, the divide and conquer or erase and replace platforms of missionaries, the boom and bust of the rubber barons, the millenarianism of false prophets, and the supposed eco-tourism of Westerners looking to unlock missing pieces in their own lives through ayahuasca-based spiritual retreats.

This is the world that we live in.

The world Arévalo fought to survive within.

The world Woodroffe killed her in.

The world Woodroffe was executed in.

Our world.

So where does this leave us? You and I.

There will be those that say none of this matters still. It could have been done better. We still need ayahuasca to heal our wounds. We deserve it.

There will be those that ask, disingenuously, if ayahuasca is off the table, then what? Where do we draw the line? What is off limits? Where does it all end?

Well, this is it. This is the line.

In response to the killing of Arévalo, the Shipi-bo-Conibo-Xetebo got together to make sure that this wouldn't be forgotten. To act on it. To refuse the lies of the retreats that parroted their name and their culture to sell feel-good spiritual adventures to lost eco-tour-ists. They called for an end to the ayahuasca tourism as an act of "spiritual extractivism." There are no questions on their part about how Woodroffe got there or why he pulled the trigger.

A union of healers: that's what they are. They re-fused the term "shaman." Rejected the concept of "sha-manism." They reclaimed their cultural memory from tourists and professionals. They were *Onanyas* once more.

That cultural memory again was recognized as a form and practice of anti-colonialist praxis.[266]

By failing to realize the history that covered the shallow grave Woodroffe was buried in, we ensure that there will be no healing. We hold tight, like Woodrof-fe, to the idea that there is a piece of ourselves that is broken. Something badly wounded. He was right about that. We are right about that. But it is not, in any case ever, something that can be solved by picking apart a new Superfood, Mystical Cure-All solution that, we believe, is buried in the cultural memory of a remote society in the Amazon.

We are all wounded. You and I. Pizarro and Woodroffe. Arévalo. Las Casas. All of us.

We don't meet at this crossroads because some of us have it figured it out. We are here precisely because none of us have.

There is no magic solution.

There is no magic pill.

There is no truth to be found in pillaging bits and pieces of different cultures throughout the world and hoping that by mashing them together we can magically make sense of things. It is civilization, it is the process of domestication itself that keeps us from a life where meaning is implicit. From living a life where we don't have to have this ridiculous existential crisis about what our place in the world is.

All of that is created. And none of it is going to make any more sense by mocking the cultural memories of others, by robbing the coping mechanisms of peoples throughout the world, as we help ourselves to a false ideal that is also our own creation: an ideal that is both a ghost of our civilization and a fabrication of it.

I don't doubt the powers of ayahuasca. I believe that we are so bound and wounded that there are experiences that a trained and knowledgeable *onanya* like Arévalo could potentially open people up with. But why is that her job? Why did Woodroffe think that over a period of years that he could suddenly learn all of this knowledge, export it back to Canada and have it make sense in a completely different context and for completely different purposes?

That's not respect. It's commodification.

Even when you remove all ethical considerations, in the assessment of anthropologist Bernd Brabec de Mori, "there is no practical reward to be expected from romanticizing and obscuring the provenance, history, and consequences of ayahuasca use."[267] In trying to create something authentic, we're hoping to find a tradition that offers some greater, universal truth. One that can be exported and used: a resource like rubber or like slaves.

Like rubber, like slaves, just when we think we've found it, just when we think we've found the thing that makes sense of everything we've done, we'll run out again. It won't work. It'll dry up and pass out of fashion. It'll be undercut by synthetics made in labs, sold by corporations.

The answer was never going to be ayahuasca.

It was never going to be in the commodification of a resource and its pillage.

That's the problem. Just as it was. Just as it is.

Civilization isn't an ethos. We tell ourselves that. It makes a nice story. But it isn't true.

Civilization is a pathology. One that is enacted by individuals. One that is carried out every single day, over and over again. It is, in Mumford's words, the original Megamachine: carried out by billions of individual human units and their machines.

We get here because the core of our needs, as social beings, as animals, are not being met. The diversion of what it means to live a life devoid of crisis management and distraction is the domestication process. Like everything else in history, it's a non-event. It has a start point and it will have an end point. But it is an on-going process. That is a process that is created and recreated daily to cater our own personal experience as a part of the Megamachine.

It is one thing to learn from other people. To understand their culture, to see how they respond to situations and circumstances. It is another to pillage that culture. Practical skills, techniques, and tools are one thing: cultural memories are another.

In the world that civilization has built, many of us are mutts and cast-offs. We are living amalgams of a history that we considered ourselves exempt from. Beneath that is a living world. It is covered in scars and in many places those scars are open wounds.

What ties us all is that we are still here. Within each of us, there is that primal anarchy. Fighting against the domestication process, yearning for a life where meaning is implicit instead of a philosophical, religious, or economical concept. We struggle for a world without resources. The world as it existed without civilization and without the systemic violence of the frontier.

It is within our reach to make that connection. To ground ourselves again. To learn to live with the earth instead of against it. To embrace our wildness.

But we cannot do that if we don't realize that the living history of this earth, our world, carries the plagues our history fostered within it. That too is living. That too is breathing.

There will be no peace of mind in this world, no transcendent inner Oneness, unless there is a direct and constant confrontation with the world that history has created. That demands that there is an understanding about our lives within the Megamachine. It demands an understanding of its inner workings, its bottlenecks, and supply lines.

It is within our reach to bleed the machine dry.

We can end the frontier. We can end the search for meaning in a broken world.

As Arévalo could have told us, it won't be easy.

But as the people of the Ucayali always remind us, missions—like civilization—are infrastructure. And infrastructure can always be destroyed and abandoned:

rendered powerless and left to rot.

Like the entombed remains of Pizarro, the bloated corpse of Fitzcarrald, the shallow grave of Woodroffe, the ghosts of our past hold strength only so long as we continue their narratives. Stories we tell ourselves to justify both our actions and inactions.

Ideas, like the people who hold them, will die in time.

If we are searching for meaning, the cultural memories that try to make sense of the colonial realities we take part in aren't ours for the taking. What is closer than all of those is the reality that each of us was born to be a nomadic hunter-gatherer. This is how we were shaped by a living history. This is how we once lived.

The primal anarchy that surges within us never had to be pretty all the time, but it works. For all the stories we like to tell, it's also the only truly egalitarian one.

I'd say that's a good starting point.

Like hunter-gatherers have always known, healing lies in community, in engaging a living history in a living world. We can't undo our past, but we do have to confront it. But that, in and of itself, is a step in the right direction. When we find ourselves within this world, then fighting for it no longer becomes an existential thought, but a necessity.

When we stop being spectators in the destruction of our world, then we can recognize the agency that we hold in our lives. We can break the patterns. We can break the Megamachine.

Instead of writing new narratives, we can make them up around fires. Sing them to the forest. Start to heal the wounds. Reshape our relationship with the world and each other.

Woodroffe came to extract a cultural memory.

Arévalo, in her life and her work, sought to root one.

In the end, the surreal reality of the frontier ensured that both were killed.

I refuse to let either be forgotten; yet it is the living history Arévalo fought for that will continue to grow. Not Woodroffe's. Her songs continue to echo throughout the Amazon in an act of defiant resistance.

Like the persistent howls of coyotes at night, one day our songs will too.

Acknowledgements

Typically a project like this takes years, if not decades. This story happened to strike on a lot of work I had been doing and particularly strong aspects of it. My original reaction came over a couple episodes of my podcast, Black and Green Podcast. I owe a bit of a nod to everyone who responded so positively to those episodes and, intentionally or not, pushed me further towards writing this book.

I owe a lot to Candice Archer for her follow up on this story and the overarching themes in particular. Also for sending a few crucial links that incidentally helped me find the entire narrative arc. Likewise, Evan Cestari has always been a massive help and in this case, lent a massive hand in research and digging when I got stuck.

I'm eternally grateful for the patience and support from the other editors of *Black and Green Review*. Most notably, the support always given by my dear friend, John Zerzan, but no less to Four Legged Human and Cliff Hayes. Joan Kovatch gave a huge hand in editing and proofing. Lilia Letsch has been massively helpful in seeing all things Black and Green through.

In no particular order, the following people have directly and indirectly been a lot of help to me during this project: Jared Ondovchik, Sloth, Joel Cimarron, Delia Turner, Alice Parman, Pegi Eyers, Parker Krieg, Peter Bauer, Dylan Garrett Smith, Gay Bradshaw, Kathryn Cardinal, Matt Moss and Slugdge for an excellent soundtrack, Jim Scheff, Will Potter, Dean Berry, and I'm sure there are others that I have missed. To them, I'm sorry, I'll catch you next round.

I have been particularly motivated by the growing decolonization movement, in everything from massive resistance to pipelines and a constant recharging of Traditional Ecological Knowledge. The continued call out against cultural appropriation demands more attention, as I hope this book makes clear.

I acknowledge that I've written this book while living on stolen Wazhazhe Manzhan (Osage) and Očeti Šakówiŋ (Sioux) land. To them, to the wildlife, to the recovering ecosystem, our resident beaver, otter, coyotes, deer, and more, I will never stop fighting civilization. And I look forward to the day my daughters might not have to either.

To Yank, I might be stubborn as hell, but I learn eventually. Thank you for everything.

For my daughters, Mica and Dyani, you continually show me why giving up is never an option. I will continue fighting for a better future for you than the one you were born into. A world where stories like this one will hopefully become a distant memory for a living world: a world finally free of civilization.

Endnotes

1. Janet Siskind, *To Hunt in the Morning*. London: Oxford University Press, 1973. Pg 188.

2. Stanley Diamond, *In Search of the Primitive*. New Brunswick: Transaction, 1987 [1974]. Pg 10.

3. Eric Wolf, *Europe and the People Without History*. Berkeley: University of California Press, 1997 [1982]. Pg 131.

4. Bryan Strong, 'Slavery and Colonialism Make Up the True Legacy of Columbus.' *New York Times*, November 4, 1989.

5. Wolf, 1997. Pgs 129 and 131.

6. Clive Ponting, *A Green History of the World*. New York: Penguin, 1991. Pg 230.

7. JR McNeill and William McNeill, *The Human Web*. New York: WW Norton, 2003. Pg 172.

8. Bartolomé de Las Casas, *A Short Account of the Destruction of the Indes*. New York: Penguin, 1992 [1552]. Pg 113.

9. Ibid. Pg 108.

10. Charles Mann, *1491*. New York: Vintage, 2006.

Pg 68.

11. John Mohawk, 'In Search of Noble Ancestors' in Christine Ward Gailey, *Civilization in Crisis: Volume* 1. Gainesville: University Press of Florida, 1992. Pg 34.

12. Dan Collyns, 'Peru's brutal murders renew focus on tourist boom for hallucinogenic brew.' *The Guardian*, April 29, 2018.

13. Richard Evan Schultes, 'Hallucinogens in the Western Hemisphere' in Peter Furst (ed), *The Flesh of the Gods: The Ritual Use of Hallucinogens*. Long Grove, IL: Waveland, 1990 [1972]. Pg 35.

14. Glenn Shepard, 'Psychoactive Plants and Ethnopsychiatric Medicines of the Matsigenka.' *Journal of Pyschoactive Drugs*. Volume 30, Number 4, Oct-Dec, 1998. Pg 326.

15. Schultes, 1990. Pg 35.

16. Ibid.

17. Collyns, 2018.

18. https://www.indiegogo.com/projects/improving-on-addiction-help#/

19. https://templeofthewayoflight.org/tragedy-in-pucallpa-the-death-of-maestra-olivia-arevalo/

20. https://templeofthewayoflight.org/retreats/ayahuasca-retreats/

21. Franklin Briceno, 'Psychedelic tourism thrives in Peru despite recent killing.' *Chicago Tribune*, June 8, 2018.

22. For more on this, see my essay 'Hooked on a Feeling' in Kevin Tucker, *Gathered Remains*. Salem, MO: Black and Green Press, 2018.

23. Sherry L. Murphy, B.S., Jiaquan Xu, M.D., Kenneth D. Kochanek, M.A., and Elizabeth Arias, Ph.D., 'Mortality in the United States, 2017.' NCHS Data Brief

No. 328, November 2018.

24. Don José Campos, *The Shaman and Ayahuasca*. Studio City, CA: Divine Arts, 2011. Pg 8.

25. Thomas King, *The Truth About Stories*. Minneapolis: University of Minnesota, 2003. Pg 113.

26. Ward Churchill, *Kill the Indian, Save the Man*. San Francisco: City Lights, 2004. Pg 14.

27. https://www.indiegogo.com/projects/improving-on-addiction-help#/

28. Ibid.

29. R Brian Ferguson, 'Blood of Leviathan.' *American Ethnologist*, Vol 17, No 2, May 1990. Pg 248.

30. Briceno, 2018.

31. Thomas Myers, 'Spanish Contacts and Social Change on the Ucayali River, Peru.' *Ethnohistory*, Vol 21, No 2, Spring 1974. Pg 135.

32. This is a criticism rightfully aimed at an early, though considerable book on the entire continent, Julian Steward and Louis Faron, *Native Peoples of South America*. New York: McGraw-Hill, 1959.

33. Warren DeBoer, 'Buffer Zones in the Cultural Ecology of Aboriginal Amazonia.' *American Antiquity*, Vol 46, No 2, April 1981; R Brian Ferguson, 'Ecological Consequences of Amazonian Warfare.' *Ethnology*, Vol 28, No 3, July 1989.

34. Charles Mann, *1493*. New York: Vintage, 2011. Pg 307. This excellent book has been an invaluable resource for piecing pieces of the larger story of the Amazon and conquest together.

35. Philip Curtin, *The World and the West*. Cambridge: Cambridge University Press, 2002. Pg 10.

36. Mann, 2011. Pgs 388-389.

37. Greg Grandin, *The Empire of Necessity*. New

York: Picador, 2014. Pgs 239-248.

38. Andrés Reséndez, *The Other Slavery*. Boston: Mariner, 2016. Pg 68.

39. Michael Williams, *Deforesting the Earth*. Chicago: University of Chicago Press, 2006. Pg 32.

40. Lucille Eakin, Erwin Lauriault and Harry Boonstra, *People of the Ucayali: The Shipibo and Conibo of Peru*. Dallas: International Museum of Cultures, 1986. Pgs 5-8.

41. For more on this, see my essay 'Society without Strangers' in Tucker, 2018.

42. Myers, 1974. Pg 146 and evidenced in the shifting placement and names in maps provided in Warren DeBoer, 'Pillage and Production in the Amazon: A View through the Conibo of the Ucayali Basin, Eastern Peru.' *World Archaeology*, Vol 18, No 2, Oct 1986.

43. Michael Brown and Eduardo Fernandez, 'Tribe and State in a Frontier Mosaic' in R Brian Ferguson and Neil Whitehead (eds), *War in the Tribal Zone*. Santa Fe: School of American Research Press, 1992. Pg 179.

44. Brown and Fernandez, 1992. Pg 179.

45. Ross Hassig, 'Aztec and Spanish Conquest in Mesoamerica' in Ferguson and Whitehead, 1992.

46. Eakin, Lauriault, and Boonstra, 1986. Pg 2.

47. Ibid.

48. DeBoer, 1986. Pg 231.

49. Ibid. Pg 233.

50. Ibid. Pg 237.

51. Ibid. Pg 238.

52. Ibid. Pg 239.

53. Ibid.

54. Myers, 1974. Pg 147.

55. Alfred Cosby, *Ecological Imperialism*. Cam-

bridge: Cambridge University Press, 2000 [1986]. Pg 196.

56. R Brian Ferguson, 'A Reexamination of the Causes of Northwest Coast Warfare' in R Brian Ferguson (ed), *Warfare, Culture, and Environment*. Orlando: Academic Press, 1984.

57. Thomas Abler, 'Beavers and Muskets' in Ferguson and Whitehead, 1992 and Francis Jennings, *The Ambiguous Iroquois Empire*. New York: WW Norton, 1984.

58. Andrew Vayda, *War in Ecological Perspective*. New York: Plenum, 1976. Pg 101. See also Andrew Vayda, *Maori Warfare*. Wellington, New Zealand: Polynesian Society, 1960.

59. Douglas Fry, *The Human Potential for Peace*. New York: Oxford University Press, 2006. Pgs 198-199.

60. Ferguson, 1990. Pg 245. See also R Brian Ferguson, *Yanomami Warfare*. Santa Fe: SARS Press, 1995 and R Brian Ferguson, 'A Savage Encounter' in Ferguson and Whitehead, 1992.

61. William Smole, *The Yanoama Indians*. Austin: University of Texas Press, 1976. Pg 31.

62. The taking and trading of shrunken heads is a massive subject, but I've touched on it elsewhere and encourage reading that as well; 'Society Without Strangers' in Tucker, 2018. Also, in showing the European fascination with heads, particularly how that led to creating a market for the head trophies taken by natives occasionally—leading to all-out endemic warfare, I strongly recommend Frances Larson, *Severed*. New York: Liveright, 2014.

63. Michael Harner, *The Jivaro*. Garden City, NY: Anchor, 1973; Daniel Steel, 'Trade Goods and Jivaro

Warfare.' *Ethnohistory*, Vol 46, No 4, Autumn 1999; and Jane Ross, 'Effects of Contact on Revenge Hostilities among the Achuarä Jivaro' in Ferguson, 1984.

64. Ponting, 1991. Pgs 117 and 218.

65. Michael Stanfield, *Red Rubber, Bleeding Trees*. Albuquerque: University of New Mexico Press, 1998.

66. Brown and Fernandez, 1992. Pgs 179-180.

67. Eakin, Lauriault and Boonstra, 1986. Pg 2.

68. DeBoer, 1986. Pg 240.

69. Ibid.

70. Eakin, Lauriault, and Boonstra, 1986. Pg 3.

71. Myers, 1974. Pg 145.

72. Eakin, Lauriault, and Boonstra, 1986. Pg 3.

73. Myers, 1974. Pg 146.

74. Eakin, Lauriault, and Boonstra, 1986.

75. DeBoer, 1981. Pg 367.

76. Paul Marcoy, *Travels in South America, Volume II*. New York: Scribner, Armstrong & Co, 1875. Pg 59.

77. Michael Taussig, *Shamanism, Colonialism, and the Wild Man*. Chicago: University of Chicago Press, 1987. Pg 134.

78. DeBoer, 1986. Pg 241.

79. Ibid.

80. Scott Wallace, *The Unconquered*. New York: Crown, 2011. Pg 208.

81. Ibid. Pgs 208-209.

82. Mann, 2011. Pg 317.

83. Stephen Harp, *A World History of Rubber*. West Sussex: John Wiley & Sons, 2016. Pg 12.

84. Mann, 2011. Pg 309.

85. Ibid. Pgs 309-314.

86. Ibid. Pg 314.

87. Eric Hobsbawn, *The Age of Empire*. New York:

Vintage, 1989. Pg 63.

88. Ibid. Pg 65.

89. Wallace, 2011. Pg 61.

90. Wolf, 1997. Pg 325.

91. Wallace, 2011. Pg 60.

92. John Charles Chasteen, *Born in Blood and Fire*. New York: WW Norton, 2001. Pg 185.

93. Taussig, 1987. Pgs 22-23.

94. Walter Hardenburg, *The Putumayo: The Devil's Paradise*. London: T Fisher Unwin, 1912. Pgs 184-185.

95. Mann, 2011. Pg 332.

96. Taussig, 1987. Pg 54.

97. Mann, 2011. Pg 332.

98. Diamond, 1987. Pg 30.

99. ED Morel, *Red Rubber*. London: National Labour Press, 1921.

100. For more on this, I strongly recommend Adam Hochschild, *King Leopold's Ghost*. Boston: Mariner, 1999.

101. Cited in John Bodley, *Victims of Progress*. Menlo Park: Cummings, 1975. Pg 32.

102. R Brian Ferguson and Neil Whitehead, 'The Violent Edge of Empire' in Ferguson and Whitehead, 1992. Pg 6.

103. Hardenburg, 1912. Pg 12.

104. Mann, 2011. Pgs 324-325.

105. Ibid. Pgs 328-329.

106. For more on this, see the excellent interview with FUNAI anthropologist Luis Felipe Torres Espinoza, 'Hunters by Choice' in *Black and Green Review* no 6. Winter 2018/2019.

107. Stefano Varese, *Salt of the Mountain: Campa Ashaninka History and Resistance in the Peruvian*

Jungle. Norman: University of Oklahoma Press, 2002 [1968]. Pgs 124-125.

108. J Valerie Fifer, 'The Empire Builders.' *Journal of Latin American Studies,* Vol 2, No 2, Nov 1970. Pgs 132-133.

109. https://en.wikipedia.org/wiki/Carlos_Ferm%C3%ADn_Fitzcarrald_Province

110. Taussig, 1987. Pg 66.

111. Ibid.

112. Myers, 1974. Pg 155.

113. S Brian Burkhalter and Robert Murphy, 'Tappers and Sappers.' *American Ethnologist,* Vol 16, No 1, February 1989. Pg 102.

114. Ibid. Pg 103.

115. Michael Edward Stanfield, *Red Rubber, Bleeding Trees.* Albuquerque: University of New Mexico Press, 1988. Pgs 40-41.

116. Burkhalter and Murphy, 1989. Pg 104.

117. Stephen Bunker, *Underdeveloping the Amazon.* Chicago: University of Chicago Press, 1990.

118. Bodley, 1975. Pg 38.

119. Cited in Taussig, 1987. Pg 66.

120. Mann, 2011. Pg 337.

121. Ibid. Pgs 337-338.

122. Ibid. Pg 339.

123. Ibid. Pg 341.

124. Taussig, 1987. Pg 67.

125. Cited in ibid.

126. Hardenburg, 1912. Pg 186.

127. Joseph Woodroffe, *The Upper Reaches of the Amazon.* London: Methuen & Co, 1914. Pg vii.

128. Michel-Rolph Trouillot, *Silencing the Past.* Boston: Beacon, 1995. Pg 114.

129. https://www.indiegogo.com/projects/improving-on-addiction-help#/

130. Myers, 1974. Pg 153.

131. Peter Roe, *The Cosmic Zygote*. New Brunswick: Rutgers University Press, 1982. Pg 35.

132. Steel, 1999. Pg 759. See also Bennett Ross, 1984.

133. Yolanda Murphy and Robert Murphy, *Women of the Forest*. New York: Columbia University Press, 2004 [1985]. Pg 31.

134. Wolf, 1997. Pg 326.

135. Ibid. Pg 329. See also Robert Murphy and Julian Steward, 'Tappers and Trappers.' *Economic Development and Cultural Change*, Vol 4, No 4, July 1956.

136. Murphy and Murphy, 2004. Pgs 31-32.

137. Ibid. Pgs 32-33.

138. Ferguson, 1995. Pg 108.

139. Ibid. Pg 105.

140. Ibid. Pgs 104-115.

141. Marcus Colchester, 'Rethinking Stone Age Economics: Some Speculations Concerning the Pre-Columbian Yanoama Economy.' *Human Ecology*, Vol 12, No 3, Sept 1984.

142. Ferguson, 1995. Pgs 113-114.

143. This one truly is a mind-blowing story, check out Greg Grandin, *Fordlandia*. New York: Picador, 2009.

144. Gerard Colby and Charlotte Dennett, *Thy Will be Done*. New York: Harper Collins, 1995. Pg 120.

145. Burkhalter and Murphy, 1989.

146. Lewis Mumford, *The Myth of the Machine*. New York: Harcourt, Brace & World, 1967. Pg 208.

147. Ferguson, 1990. Pg 245.

148. Peter Worsley, *The Trumpet Shall Sound.* New

York: Shocken Books, 1968. Pg 11.

149. Ibid. Pg 44.

150. Norman Cohn, *The Pursuit of the Millennium*. New York: Oxford University Press, 1970 [1961]. Pg 15.

151. Varese, 2002. Pg 88.

152. Ibid.

153. Ibid.

154. Ibid. Pg 87.

155. Cited in ibid. Pg 89.

156. Ibid. Pgs 89-90.

157. Ibid. Pg 91.

158. Cited in ibid.

159. Ibid. Pgs 91-92.

160. Ibid. Pgs 98-99.

161. Ibid. Pg 105.

162. Ibid. Pg 96.

163. Ibid. Pg 107.

164. Brown and Fernandez, 1992. Pg 182.

165. Ibid.

166. Ibid. Pg 184.

167. Ibid. Pg 185.

168. Varese, 2002. Pg 126.

169. Brown and Fernandez, 1992. Pg 188.

170. Cited in Bernd Barbec de Mori, 'Tracing Hallucinations' in Hendrik Jungaberle and Beatriz Labate (eds), *The Internalization of Ayahuasca*. Zurich: LIT-Verlag, 2011. Pg 23.

171. Kenneth Tupper, 'The Globalization of Ayahuasca.' *International Journal of Drug Policy.* Volume 19, 2008. Pg 298.

172. Dennis McKenna and Jordi Riba, 'New World Tryptamine Hallucinogens and the Nueroscience of Ayahuasca' in Halberstadt, Vollenweider, and Nichols

(eds) *Behavioral Neurobiology of Psychedelic Drugs. Current Topics in Behavioral Neurosciences*, vol 36. Berlin: Springer, 2016.

173. De Mori, 2011. Pg 24.

174. Tucker, 2018. Pgs 92-105.

175. Rafael Lanaro, et al, 'Ritualistic Use of Ayahuasca versus Street Use of Similar Substances Seized by the Police.' *Journal of Psychoactive Drugs*, Vol 47, No 2. Apr-June, 2015. Pg 136.

176. Schultes, 1990. Pg 35.

177. Gerardo Reichel-Dolmatoff, 'The Cultural Context of an Aboriginal Hallucinogen; *Banisteriopsis Caapi'* in Furst, 1990. Pg 87.

178. Stephen Hugh-Jones, 'Shamans, Prophets, Priests, and Pastors' in Nicholas Thomas and Caroline Humphrey (eds), *Shamanism, History, and the State.* Ann Arbor: University of Michigan Press, 1994.

179. Schultes, 1990. Pg 35.

180. Peter Gow, 'River People' in Thomas and Humphrey, 1994. Pg 92.

181. De Mori, 2011. Pgs 32-33.

182. Ibid. Pg 33.

183. Richard Katz, *Boiling Energy*. Cambridge: Harvard University Press, 1982. Pg 35.

184. David Riches, 'Shamanism: The Key to Religion.' *Man,* New Series, Vol 29, No 2, June 1994. Pg 382.

185. Gerardo Reichel-Dolmatoff, 'Cosmology as Ecological Analysis.' *Man,* New Series, Vol 11, No 3, September 1976. Pg 315.

186. Kenneth Good with David Chanoff, *Into the Heart.* New York: Simon and Schuster, 1991. Pg 68.

187. Laurent Rivier and Jan-Erik Lindgren, '"Ayahuasca," the South American Hallucinogenic Drink.'

Economic Botany, Vol 26, No 2, Apr-Jan, 1972. Pg 102.

188. Gow, 1994. Pg 91.

189. Clayton and Carole Robarchek, 'The Aucas, the Cannibals, and the Missionaries' in Thomas Gregor (ed), *A Natural History of Peace*. Nashville: Vanderbilt University Press, 1996. Pg 197.

190. Clayton Robarchek and Carole Robarchek, *Waorani: The Contexts of Violence and War*. For Worth: Harcourt Brace, 1988. Pg 106.

191. Laura Rival, *Trekking Through History*. New York: Columbia University Press, 2002. Pg 79.

192. Robarcheck and Robarcheck, 1988. Pg 112.

193. Miguel Alexiandes and Daniela Peluso, 'Plants 'of the Ancestors,' Plants 'of the Outsiders' in Alexiandes (ed), *Mobility and Migration in Indigenous Amazonia*. New York: Berghahn, 2009. Pgs 235-236.

194. Shepard, 1998. Pg 326.

195. De Mori, 2011. Pg 31.

196. Ibid. Pgs 33-34.

197. Gow, 1994. Pg 107.

198. Tupper, 2008. Pg 299.

199. http://www.afamiliajuramidam.org/english/mestre_irineu_english.htm The website is written and maintained by Irineu's followers, so be prepared for crazy.

200. Tupper, 2008. Pg 299.

201. Ibid.

202. Gow, 1994. Pg 111.

203. Lanaro, et al, 2015. Pg 133.

204. Gow, 1994. Pg 105.

205. Ibid. Pg 106.

206. Ibid. Pg 99.

207. Ibid. Pg 100.

208. Ibid. Pg 101.

209. "Historical sorcery" is a term from Taussig. Ibid. Pg 104.

210. Ibid. Pg 96.

211. John Zerzan, *Future Primitive*. Brooklyn: Autonomedia, 1994. Pgs 45-46.

212. This deserves so much more attention. In Canada and the US, there is a campaign focused on the plague of "Missing and Murdered Indigenous Women." Many of whom are killed brutally and their murders are not only left unsolved, but wantonly disregarded. It runs off of a generalized and active disinterest in confronting the realities of contemporary forms of racism that breed murderers and also teach racists that "dead Indians" still don't get any respect in the eyes of the law. There are a couple really good podcasts covering this, particularly *Missing and Murdered* by the CBC. I also strongly recommend the Canadaland mini-series, *Thunder Bay*.

213. https://globalnews.ca/news/4161139/sebastian-woodroffe-killed-mob-peru/ Note that the flier is in the video, but, *fair warning*, some of the lynching footage is in there too.

214. Bernd Barbec de Mori, 'From the Native's Point of View' in Beatriz Caiuby Labate and Clancy Caunar, *Ayahuasca Shamanism in the Amazon and Beyond*. Oxford: Oxford University Press, 2014. Pg 221.

215. De Mori, 2014. Pg 221.

216. Ibid. Pg 214.

217. Gow, 1994. Pg 103.

218. Rivier and Lindgren, 1972. Pg 110.

219. This is a primary subject of another book I am currently writing, *Of Gods and Country: the Domestica-*

tion of the World. It is sickening how much the role of missionaries has gone unnoticed and unreported in the process of colonization.

220. Pierre Clastres, *Archeology of Violence*. Los Angeles: Semiotext(e), 2010 [1980]. Pg 108.

221. Kenneth Mills, 'Religious Coercion in Midcolonial Peru' in John Schwaller (ed), *The Church in Colonial Latin America*. Wilmington, DE: Scholarly Resources, 2000. Pg 149.

222. An excellent look into this is from a former missionary, Daniel Everett, *Don't Sleep There are Snakes*. New York: Pantheon, 2008.

223. This is a major focus in my work-in-progress, *Of Gods and Country*, but it's a massive and important subject. Just a sampling of books worth looking into; Churchill, 2004; Celia Haig-Brown, *Resistance and Renewal: Surviving the Indian Residential School*. Vancouver: Tillacum Library, 1988; Shelagh Rogers, Mike DeGagné, Jonathan Dewar, and Glen Lowry (eds), *Speaking my Truth*. Ottowa: Aboriginal Healing Foundation, 2012; and Theodore Fontaine, *Broken Circle*. Victoria: Heritage House, 2010.

224. For example, see Trace Hentz (ed), *Stolen Generations*. Greenfield, MA: Blue Hand, 2016.

225. Jo Woodman and Alicia Kroemer, 'There are Hundreds of Thousands of Indigenous Children in Residential Schools Around the World Today.' *Intercontinental Cry*, Sept 28, 2018.

226. Norman Lewis, *The Missionaries*. New York: McGraw-Hill, 1988. Pg 21.

227. Ibid. Pg 23.

228. De Mori, 2011. Pg 28.

229. Hugh Brody, *The Other Side of Eden*. New York:

North End, 2000. Pg 231.

230. Nearly all illnesses carried by the colonizers are the product of domestication, particularly living in proximity to domesticated animals raised in confinement. See Mark Nathan Cohen, *Health and the Rise of Civilization*. New Haven, CT: Yale, 1991.

231. Chellis Glendinning, *My Name is Chellis and I'm in Recovery from Western Civilization*. Boston: Shambhala, 1994.

232. Paul Shepard, *Nature and Madness*. San Francisco: Sierra Club, 1982.

233. GA Bradshaw, *Carnivore Minds*. New Haven, CT: Yale, 2017. Pg 217.

234. Op Cit.

235. Cited in GA Bradshaw, *Elephants on the Edge*. New Haven, CT: Yale, 2009. Pg 160.

236. Cited in Wendy Rose, 'The Great Pretenders' in M. Annette Jaimes (ed), *The State of Native America*. Boston: South End, 1992. Pg 403.

237. Geary Hobson, 'The Rise of the White Shaman as a New Version of Cultural Imperialism' in Geary Hobson (ed), *The Remembered Earth*. Albuquerque: University of New Mexico Press, 1979.

238. Leslie Marmon Silko, 'An Old-Time Indian Attack Conducted in Two Parts' in Hobson, 1979. Pg 213.

239. Ibid. Pg 215.

240. Geary Hobson, 'The Rise of the White Shaman: Twenty-Five Years Later.' *Studies in American Indian Literatures*, Series 2, Vol 14, No 2/3. Summer/Fall 2002. Pg 5.

241. Ibid. Pg 6.

242. Lisa Aldred, 'Plastic Shamans and Astroturf Sun Dances.' *The American Indian Quarterly*. Vol 24,

No 3. Summer 2000. Pgs 329-330.

243. Collyns, 2018.

244. Samantha Schmidt and Avi Selk, 'Arrests loom after Peruvian villagers 'lynch' tourist accused of killing their shaman.' *The Washington Post*, April 24, 2018.

245. De Mori, 2014. Pgs 207-208.

246. Ibid. Pg 208.

247. De Mori, 2011. Pg 33.

248. Gow, 1994. Pg 95.

249. De Mori, 2014. Pgs 218-219.

250. Steel, 1999. Pg 761.

251. De Mori, 2011. Pg 44.

252. Ibid.

253. De Mori, 2014. Pg 222.

254. Ibid. Pg 223.

255. Ibid. Pg 224.

256. Ibid. Pg 220.

257. Ibid. Pg 225.

258. Ibid. Pg 226.

259. Max Oprey, 'Tourist boom for ayahuasca a mixed blessing for Amazon.' *The Guardian*, January 24, 2017.

260. Jeremy Cherfas, 'Your Quinoa Habit Really Did Help Peru's Poor. But There's Trouble Ahead.' *NPR*, March 31, 2016.

261. Adrienne K, 'Sephora's "Starter Witch Kit" and Spiritual Theft.' *Native Appropriations*. September 5, 2018. Online at: https://nativeappropriations.com/2018/09/sephoras-starter-witch-kit-and-spiritual-theft.html

262. Philippe Descola, *Spears of Twilight*. New York: New Press, 1996. Pg 206.

263. Shepard, 1998. Pg 330.

264. Kenneth Tupper, 'Ayahuasca Healing Beyond the Amazon.' *Global Networks*, Vol 9, No 1, January 2009.

265. https://theshiftnetwork.com/ShamanicJourneying

266. The Shipibo Conibo Center of New York, 'In the Declaration of Yarinacocha, Shipibo Healers Organize To Resist Spiritual Extractivism.' http://realitysandwich.com/323245/in-the-declaration-of-yarinacocha-shipibo-healers-organize-to-resist-spiritual-extractivism/

267. De Mori, 2011. Pg 45.

Bibliography

Abler, Thomas
   -'Beavers and Muskets' in Ferguson and White-
   head, 1992
Aldred, Lisa
   -'Plastic Shamans and Astroturf Sun Dances.' *The*
   American Indian Quarterly. Vol 24, No 3. Summer
   2000.
Alexiandes, Miguel
   -(ed) *Mobility and Migration in Indigenous Amazo-*
   nia. New York: Berghahn, 2009.
Alexiandes, Miguel and Peluso, Daniela
   -'Plants 'of the Ancestors,' Plants 'of the Outsiders'
   in Alexiandes (ed), *Mobility and Migration in In-*
   digenous Amazonia. New York: Berghahn, 2009.
Briceno, Franklin
   -'Psychedelic tourism thrives in Peru despite recent
   killing.' *Chicago Tribune*, June 8, 2018.
Bodley, John
   -*Victims of Progress*. Menlo Park: Cummings, 1975.
Bradshaw, GA

-*Elephants on the Edge*. New Haven, CT: Yale, 2009.
-*Carnivore Minds*. New Haven, CT: Yale, 2017.

Brody, Hugh
-*The Other Side of Eden*. New York: North End, 2000.

Brown, Michael and Fernandez, Eduardo
-'Tribe and State in a Frontier Mosaic' in Ferguson and Whitehead, 1992.

Bunker, Stephen
-*Underdeveloping the Amazon*. Chicago: University of Chicago Press, 1990.

Burkhalter, S Brian and Murphy, Robert
-'Tappers and Sappers.' *American Ethnologist*, Vol 16, No 1, February 1989.

Campos, Don José
-*The Shaman and Ayahuasca*. Studio City, CA: Divine Arts, 2011.

Chasteen, John Charles
-*Born in Blood and Fire*. New York: WW Norton, 2001.

Cherfas, Jeremy
-'Your Quinoa Habit Really Did Help Peru's Poor. But There's Trouble Ahead.' *NPR*, March 31, 2016.

Churchill, Ward
-*Kill the Indian, Save the Man*. San Francisco: City Lights, 2004.

Clastres, Pierre
-*Archeology of Violence*. Los Angeles: Semiotext(e), 2010 [1980].

Cohen, Mark Nathan
-*Health and the Rise of Civilization*. New Haven, CT: Yale, 1991.

Cohn, Norman

-*The Pursuit of the Millennium.* New York: Oxford University Press, 1970 [1961].

Colby, Gerard and Dennett, Charlotte
-*Thy Will be Done.* New York: Harper Collins, 1995.

Colchester, Marcus
-'Rethinking Stone Age Economics: Some Speculations Concerning the Pre-Columbian Yanoama Economy.' *Human Ecology*, Vol 12, No 3, Sept 1984.

Collyns, Dan
-'Peru's brutal murders renew focus on tourist boom for hallucinogenic brew.' *The Guardian*, April 29, 2018.

Cosby, Alfred
-*Ecological Imperialism.* Cambridge: Cambridge University Press, 2000 [1986].

Curtin, Philip
-*The World and the West.* Cambridge: Cambridge University Press, 2002.

de Las Casas, Bartolomé
-*A Short Account of the Destruction of the Indes.* New York: Penguin, 1992 [1552].

DeBoer, Warren
-'Buffer Zones in the Cultural Ecology of Aboriginal Amazonia.' *American Antiquity*, Vol 46, No 2, April 1981.
-'Pillage and Production in the Amazon: A View through the Conibo of the Ucayali Basin, Eastern Peru.' *World Archaeology*, Vol 18, No 2, Oct 1986.

de Mori, Bernd Barbec
-'Tracing Hallucinations' in Jungaberle and Labate, 2011.
-'From the Native's Point of View' in Labate and Caunar, 2014.

Descola, Philippe
   -*Spears of Twilight*. New York: New Press, 1996.
Diamond, Stanley
   -*In Search of the Primitive*. New Brunswick: Transaction, 1987 [1974].
Eakin, Lucille, Lauriault, Erwin and Boonstra, Harry
   -*People of the Ucayali: The Shipibo and Conibo of Peru*. Dallas: International Museum of Cultures, 1986.
Espinoza, Luis Felipe Torres
   -'Hunters by Choice' in *Black and Green Review* no 6. Winter 2019.
Everett, Daniel
   -*Don't Sleep There are Snakes*. New York: Pantheon, 2008.
Ferguson, R Brian
   -(ed) *Warfare, Culture, and Environment*. Orlando: Academic Press, 1984.
   -'A Reexamination of the Causes of Northwest Coast Warfare' in Ferguson, 1984.
   -'Ecological Consequences of Amazonian Warfare.' *Ethnology*, Vol 28, No 3, July 1989.
   -'Blood of Leviathan.' *American Ethnologist*, Vol 17, No 2, May 1990.
   -'A Savage Encounter' in Ferguson and Whitehead, 1992.
   -*Yanomami Warfare*. Santa Fe: SARS Press, 1995.
Ferguson, R Brian and Whitehead, Neil
   -(eds) *War in the Tribal Zone*. Santa Fe: School of American Research Press, 1992.
   -'The Violent Edge of Empire' in Ferguson and Whitehead, 1992.
Fifer, J Valerie

-'The Empire Builders.' *Journal of Latin American Studies*, Vol 2, No 2, Nov 1970.

Fontaine, Theodore
-*Broken Circle*. Victoria: Heritage House, 2010.

Fry, Douglas
-*The Human Potential for Peace*. New York: Oxford University Press, 2006.

Furst, Peter
-(ed) *The Flesh of the Gods: The Ritual Use of Hallucinogens*. Long Grove, IL: Waveland, 1990 [1972].

Gailey, Christine Ward
-(ed) *Civilization in Crisis: Volume* 1. Gainesville: University Press of Florida, 1992.

Glendinning, Chellis
-*My Name is Chellis and I'm in Recovery from Western Civilization*. Boston: Shambhala, 1994.

Good, Kenneth and Chanoff, David
-*Into the Heart*. New York: Simon and Schuster, 1991.

Gow, Peter
-'River People' in Thomas and Humphrey, 1994.

Grandin, Greg
-*Fordlandia*. New York: Picador, 2009.
-*The Empire of Necessity*. New York: Picador, 2014.

Gregor, Thomas
-(ed) *A Natural History of Peace*. Nashville: Vanderbilt University Press, 1996.

Haig-Brown, Celia
-*Resistance and Renewal: Surviving the Indian Residential School*. Vancouver: Tillacum Library, 1988.

Halberstadt, Vollenweider, and Nichols
-(eds) *Behavioral Neurobiology of Psychedelic Drugs. Current Topics in Behavioral Neurosciences*,

vol 36. Berlin: Springer, 2016.

Hardenburg, Walter

-*The Putumayo: The Devil's Paradise*. London: T Fisher Unwin, 1912.

Harner, Michael

-*The Jivaro*. Garden City, NY: Anchor, 1973.

Harp, Stephen

-*A World History of Rubber*. West Sussex: John Wiley & Sons, 2016.

Hassig, Ross

-Aztec and Spanish Conquest in Mesoamerica' in Ferguson and Whitehead, 1992.

Hentz, Trace

-(ed) *Stolen Generations*. Greenfield, MA: Blue Hand, 2016.

Hobsbawn, Eric

-*The Age of Empire*. New York: Vintage, 1989.

Hobson, Geary

-(ed) *The Remembered Earth*. Albuquerque: University of New Mexico Press, 1979.

-'The Rise of the White Shaman as a New Version of Cultural Imperialism' in Hobson, 1979.

-'The Rise of the White Shaman: Twenty-Five Years Later.' *Studies in American Indian Literatures*, Series 2, Vol 14, No 2/3. Summer/Fall 2002.

Hochschild, Adam

-*King Leopold's Ghost*. Boston: Mariner, 1999.

Hugh-Jones, Stephen

-'Shamans, Prophets, Priests, and Pastors' in Thomas and Humphrey, 1994.

Jaimes, M. Annette

-(ed) *The State of Native America*. Boston: South End, 1992.

Jennings, Francis
-*The Ambiguous Iroquois Empire*. New York: WW Norton, 1984.

Jungaberle, Hendrik and Labate, Beatriz
-(eds) *The Internalization of Ayahuasca*. Zurich: LIT-Verlag, 2011.

Katz, Richard
-*Boiling Energy*. Cambridge: Harvard University Press, 1982.

King, Thomas
-*The Truth About Stories*. Minneapolis: University of Minnesota, 2003.

Labate, Beatriz Caiuby and Caunar, Clancy
-*Ayahuasca Shamanism in the Amazon and Beyond*. Oxford: Oxford University Press, 2014.

Lanaro, Rafael, et al,
-'Ritualistic Use of Ayahuasca versus Street Use of Similar Substances Seized by the Police.' *Journal of Psychoactive Drugs,* Vol 47, No 2. Apr-June 2015.

Larson, Frances
-*Severed*. New York: Liveright, 2014.

Lewis, Norman
-*The Missionaries*. New York: McGraw-Hill, 1988.

Mann, Charles
-*1491*. New York: Vintage, 2006.
-*1493*. New York: Vintage, 2011.

Marcoy, Paul
-*Travels in South America, Volume II*. New York: Scribner, Armstrong & Co, 1875.

McKenna, Dennis and Riba, Jordi
-'New World Tryptamine Hallucinogens and the Nueroscience of Ayahuasca' in Halberstadt, Vollenweider, and Nichols, 2016.

McNeill, JR and McNeill, William
  -*The Human Web*. New York: WW Norton, 2003.
Mills, Kenneth
  -'Religious Coercion in Midcolonial Peru' in John
  Schwaller (ed), *The Church in Colonial Latin Amer-
  ica*. Wilmington, DE: Scholarly Resources, 2000.
Mohawk, John
  -'In Search of Noble Ancestors' in Gailey, 1992.
Morel, ED
  -*Red Rubber*. London: National Labour Press, 1921.
Mumford, Lewis
  -*The Myth of the Machine*. New York: Harcourt,
  Brace & World, 1967.
Murphy, Robert and Steward, Julian
  -'Tappers and Trappers.' *Economic Development
  and Cultural Change*, Vol 4, No 4, July 1956.
Murphy, Sherry L. B.S., Xu, Jiaquan M.D., Kochanek,
  Kenneth D. M.A., and Arias, Elizabeth Ph.D.,
  -'Mortality in the United States, 2017.' NCHS Data
  Brief No. 328, November 2018.
Murphy, Yolanda and Murphy, Robert
  -*Women of the Forest*. New York: Columbia Uni-
  versity Press, 2004 [1985].
Myers, Thomas
  -'Spanish Contacts and Social Change on the Ucay-
  ali River, Peru.' *Ethnohistory*, Vol 21, No 2, Spring
  1974.
Oprey, Max
  -'Tourist boom for ayahuasca a mixed blessing for
  Amazon.' *The Guardian*, January 24, 2017.
Ponting, Clive
  -*A Green History of the World*. New York: Penguin,
  1991.

Reichel-Dolmatoff, Gerardo
-'Cosmology as Ecological Analysis.' *Man,* New Series, Vol 11, No 3, September 1976.
-'The Cultural Context of an Aboriginal Hallucinogen; *Banisteriopsis Caapi'* in Furst, 1990.

Reséndez, Andrés
-*The Other Slavery.* Boston: Mariner, 2016.

Riches, David
-'Shamanism: The Key to Religion.' *Man,* New Series, Vol 29, No 2, June 1994.

Rival, Laura
-*Trekking Through History.* New York: Columbia University Press, 2002.

Rivier, Laurent and Lindgren, Jan-Erik
-'"Ayahuasca," the South American Hallucinogenic Drink.' *Economic Botany,* Vol 26, No 2, Apr-Jan, 1972.

Robarchek, Clayton and Carole
-*Waorani: The Contexts of Violence and War.* For Worth: Harcourt Brace, 1988.
-'The Aucas, the Cannibals, and the Missionaries' in Gregor, 1996.

Roe, Peter
-*The Cosmic Zygote.* New Brunswick: Rutgers University Press, 1982.

Rogers, Shelagh, DeGagné, Mike, Dewar, Jonathan and Lowry, Glen
-(eds) *Speaking my Truth.* Ottowa: Aboriginal Healing Foundation, 2012.

Rose, Wendy
-'The Great Pretenders' in Jaimes, 1992.

Ross, Jane
-'Effects of Contact on Revenge Hostilities among

the Achuarä Jivaro' in Ferguson, 1984.

Schmidt, Samantha and Selk, Avi

'-Arrests loom after Peruvian villagers 'lynch' tourist accused of killing their shaman.' *The Washington Post*, April 24, 2018.

Schultes, Richard Evan

-'Hallucinogens in the Western Hemisphere' in Furst, 1990.

Schwaller, John

-(ed) *The Church in Colonial Latin America*. Wilmington, DE: Scholarly Resources, 2000.

Shepard, Glenn

-'Psychoactive Plants and Ethnopsychiatric Medicines of the Matsigenka.' *Journal of Pyschoactive Drugs*. Volume 30, Number 4, Oct-Dec, 1998

Shepard, Paul

-*Nature and Madness*. San Francisco: Sierra Club, 1982.

Silko, Leslie Marmon

-'An Old-Time Indian Attack Conducted in Two Parts' in Hobson, 1979.

Siskind, Janet

-*To Hunt in the Morning*. London: Oxford University Press, 1973.

Smole, William

-*The Yanoama Indians*. Austin: University of Texas Press, 1976.

Stanfield, Michael

-*Red Rubber, Bleeding Trees*. Albuquerque: University of New Mexico Press, 1998.

Steel, Daniel

-'Trade Goods and Jivaro Warfare.' *Ethnohistory*, Vol 46, No 4, Autumn 1999.

Steward, Julian and Faron, Louis
-*Native Peoples of South America*. New York: Mc-Graw-Hill, 1959.

Strong, Bryan
-'Slavery and Colonialism Make Up the True Legacy of Columbus.' *New York Times*, November 4, 1989.

Taussig, Michael
-*Shamanism, Colonialism, and the Wild Man*. Chicago: University of Chicago Press, 1987.

Thomas, Nicholas and Humphrey, Caroline
-(eds) *Shamanism, History, and the State*. Ann Arbor: University of Michigan Press, 1994.

Trouillot, Michel-Rolph
-*Silencing the Past*. Boston: Beacon, 1995.

Tucker, Kevin
-*Gathered Remains*. Salem, MO: Black and Green Press, 2018.

Tupper, Kenneth
-'The Globalization of Ayahuasca.' *International Journal of Drug Policy*. Volume 19, 2008.
-'Ayahuasca Healing Beyond the Amazon.' *Global Networks*, Vol 9, No 1, January 2009.

Varese, Stefano
-*Salt of the Mountain: Campa Ashaninka History and Resistance in the Peruvian Jungle*. Norman: University of Oklahoma Press, 2002 [1968].

Vayda, Andrew
-*Maori Warfare*. Wellington, New Zealand: Polynesian Society, 1960.
-*War in Ecological Perspective*. New York: Plenum, 1976.

Wallace, Scott

-*The Unconquered*. New York: Crown, 2011.

Williams, Michael
-*Deforesting the Earth*. Chicago: University of Chicago Press, 2006.

Wolf, Eric
-*Europe and the People Without History*. Berkeley: University of California Press, 1997 [1982].

Woodman, Jo and Kroemer, Alicia
-'There are Hundreds of Thousands of Indigenous Children in Residential Schools Around the World Today.' *Intercontinental Cry*, Sept 28, 2018.

Woodroffe, Joseph
-*The Upper Reaches of the Amazon*. London: Methuen & Co, 1914.

Worsley, Peter
-*The Trumpet Shall Sound*. New York: Shocken Books, 1968.

Zerzan, John
-*Future Primitive*. Brooklyn: Autonomedia, 1994.

About the Author

Kevin Tucker is a primal anarchist writer, rewilding human, and father. He is the author of *For Wildness and Anarchy* (Black and Green Press, 2010) and *Gathered Remains* (Black and Green Press, 2018). He was the editor of *Species Traitor: an Insurrectionary Anarcho-Primitivist Journal* (2000-2005), founder of the Black and Green Network, was a regular contributor of *Green Anarchy* (2000-2008), and is the founding co-editor of *Black and Green Review* (2015-). He hosts the Black and Green Podcast. He lives in the Ozarks of central Missouri.

kevintucker.org
primalanarchy.org